ENDORSEMENTS

Touchstones captures a lifetime of experience running successful businesses and is condensed into an extremely useful and easy-to-remember format. Joe has managed to replicate the way he successfully operated as a CEO, board member, and chair of various companies into an extremely useful reference guide for managers and leaders at all levels. His use of a one liner (or touchstone) captures the concept as well as the attention of the reader and at the same time displays a little of Joe's personality. This flows logically into an explanation of the thought process, which brings the subject to life. Throughout his book, Joe draws on the principles of many scholars of business such as Drucker, Porter, and others, but what *Touchstones* accomplishes is based more on reality than theory and as such is likely more useful as day-to-day reference material by experienced and aspiring managers and leaders alike.

— **Nick Green**
President and CEO, Avid Bioservices

This book represents a great compilation of lifelong experiences and lessons learned. I really like the takeaways at the end of each section which provide a "go to" reference for most situations and reminders of key leadership traits. A must-read and reference for future and current leaders.

— Dave Bender
President, AvtechTyee Corporation

In business, just about every mistake has already been made by someone. Great leaders and executives figure out those mistakes and avoid making them. Joe has provided a superb tool to help you navigate away from those all-too-common professional and personal pitfalls. Read away.

— Paul Manning
Chairman, President and CEO, Sensient Technologies Corp.

Dr. Carleone, a proven industry leader with many years of experience in diverse industries, has summarized his learnings into a very simple, easy-to-read guide for business leaders. Internalizing the concepts associated with the "45 Touchstones" will allow leaders to navigate through the complexities of business and will make a lasting difference in their careers and personal lives. This book is a must-read for all current and future business leaders.

— Dr. Aslam Malik
CEO, SK Pharmteco and AMPAC Fine Chemicals

Whilst most leadership books contain some new insights and ah-ha moments for the aspiring leader, this book brings together a cornucopia of leadership wisdom distilled from the author's own experiences and from studying the work of others in the field to provide a guide for self-improvement and further study for any business leader.

— Mark R. Bamforth

Entrepreneur, mentor, and investor in life science

The Touchstones of Leadership is a fabulous book—very readable, thoroughly researched. It reveals that great leadership requires both leading and managing skills, but first and foremost the foundation of good leadership is the ability to manage oneself. Joe has distilled great management and leadership wisdom from his extensive industry experience and has captured them as "touchstones," gems of leadership and management which are as timeless as they are necessary to any successful organization. *Touchstones* presents a comprehensive, yet concise, leadership model that brings together the essential softer, interpersonal skills with the strategic and execution skills so necessary to become an effective leader in the business world. It is easily digestible and summarized in "index cards" for later review.

—William Readdy

US Navy Test Pilot, NASA Astronaut, NASA Senior Executive

The TOUCHSTONES *of* LEADERSHIP

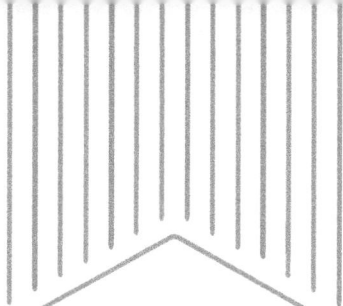

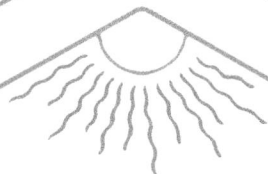

JOSEPH CARLEONE

The
TOUCHSTONES
of
LEADERSHIP

ESSENTIAL PRINCIPLES
for BUSINESS LEADERS

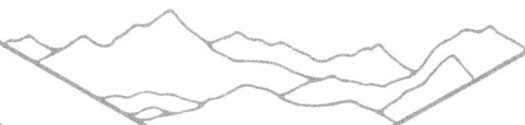

Forbes | Books

Published by Forbes Books, Charleston, South Carolina.
An imprint of Advantage Media Group.

Forbes Books is a registered trademark, and the Forbes Books colophon is a trademark of Forbes Media, LLC.

Printed in the United States of America.

10 9 8 7 6 5 4 3 2 1

ISBN: 979-8-88750-530-5 (Hardcover)
ISBN: 979-8-88750-531-2 (eBook)

Library of Congress Control Number: 2024906391

Cover design by Lance Buckley.
Layout design by Ruthie Wood.

This custom publication is intended to provide accurate information and the opinions of the author in regard to the subject matter covered. It is sold with the understanding that the publisher, Forbes Books, is not engaged in rendering legal, financial, or professional services of any kind. If legal advice or other expert assistance is required, the reader is advised to seek the services of a competent professional.

Since 1917, Forbes has remained steadfast in its mission to serve as the defining voice of entrepreneurial capitalism. Forbes Books, launched in 2016 through a partnership with Advantage Media, furthers that aim by helping business and thought leaders bring their stories, passion, and knowledge to the forefront in custom books. Opinions expressed by Forbes Books authors are their own. To be considered for publication, please visit **books.Forbes.com**.

To Mom and Dad

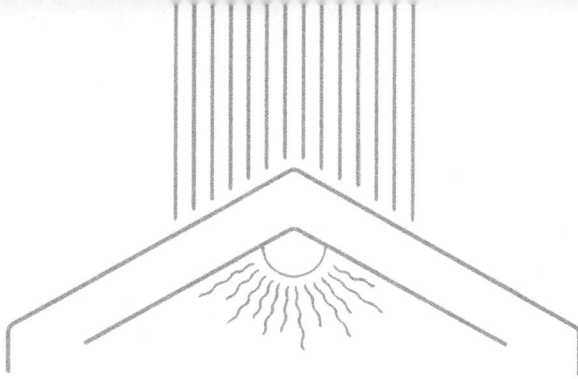

CONTENTS

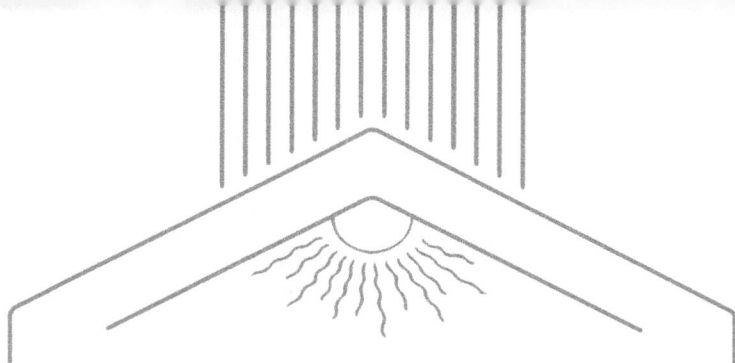

PREFACE

With the first half of my career in aerospace and defense and the second half in the pharmaceutical manufacturing and services business, I was lucky to experience many leadership lessons.

I have experienced leadership positions in armament systems, smart munitions, space surveillance satellites, solid and liquid rocket propulsion, specialty chemicals, pharmaceutical active ingredients, and biological pharmaceuticals. I started using short one-liners in staff meetings, program reviews, and problem-solving sessions to make a point. And as I did, one of my staff suggested I start writing these down.

After compiling a list and culling it to select the most salient ones, I wound up with forty-five keepers I call "Touchstones." These one-liners are guidelines to help business leaders navigate business streams as they flow. In search of a model to structure these touchstones, I realized leadership required four aspects:

- managing oneself

- interpersonal skills

- management skills

- strategic perspective

This comprehensive model covers the continuum and connectivity in leading and managing a business. Great business leaders are challenged to do both. This model was the breakthrough needed to create a complete view of leadership and organize the Touchstones in a logical manner. These Touchstones are the basis of a leadership course I have presented to several leadership teams from both large and small companies. And this book grew out of my experience in preparing and teaching this leadership course.

I sincerely thank Dr. Aslam Malik for first suggesting I compile a list of these one-liners and our many discussions about their meaning and applicability. I also thank the many participants in the Touchstones courses for their excellent feedback in helping me shape the content and structure of this book. I am sincerely indebted to Reverend Joseph Campellone for his mentorship and for encouraging me to "write down my thoughts" on leadership during our discussions. Thanks are also due to the many associates, colleagues, bosses, and collaborators throughout my education and career who have influenced my thinking on leadership. Furthermore, I thank the staff of Forbes Books for their excellent feedback and help in bringing this book to life.

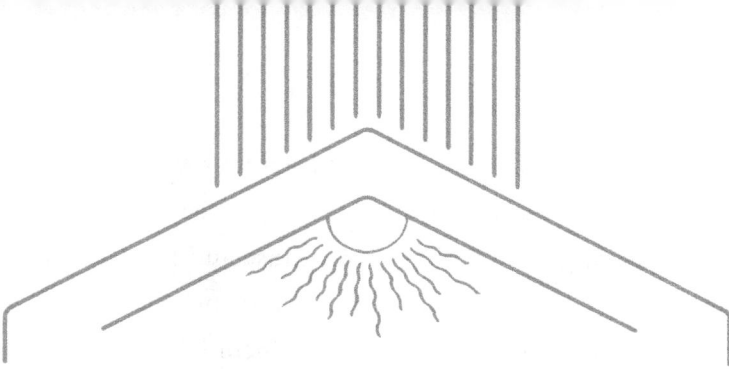

INTRODUCTION

Laying the Foundation

In business, it is critical that leaders not only lead but also effectively manage. This raises the question: How can *leaders* become great if they do not have the management problem-solving skills and planning capabilities necessary to challenge, review, evaluate, and approve a forecast or business investment that is proposed? Similarly, how can *managers* become great if they do not have an overall view and understanding of the market, competition, technology, and differentiators to buy into the strategic direction of the business?

If we ascribe to the well-known statement that "management is doing things right; leadership is doing the right things,"[1] then one can conclude that business leaders must lead *and* manage. Therefore, we should not think about leaders and managers as different people. We must coach our staff to lead when necessary and manage when critical (Bailey, 2022).[2]

---

1   This is often attributed to Peter Drucker. There is debate about this since there is only a claim that it was overheard that he said this. We know that Drucker stated, "Efficiency is doing things right; effectiveness is doing the right things."

2   Information in brackets throughout the book refers to sources listed in the Bibliography, which are arranged alphabetically by the author.

Leadership has often been defined with a focus on style. Many attribute the label "leader" to charismatic or visionary people who inspire a following for a highly visible cause and place the leader at the pinnacle of it. For example, when one mentions leadership, the names of George Washington, Abraham Lincoln, Winston Churchill, Martin Luther King Jr., and Nelson Mandela often immediately enter the discussion. Leadership, however, is also demonstrated in everyday life, such as at work, home, and volunteer roles.

Another common approach to understanding leadership is recounting influential business leaders' stories. We examine their decisive actions that have resulted in successful outcomes and use these examples to see how they can apply to our business. Unfortunately, these actions are typically not universal and only apply to some situations.

> In business, it is critical that leaders not only lead but also effectively manage.

I have found that every company is unique. A better approach to understanding leadership is to look at how these very successful leaders think. Research has shown that exceptional leaders can entertain two opposing ideas and continue to evaluate them effectively (Martin, 2007). This process has been called *integrative thinking* and is a critical factor in exceptional leadership.

Leadership can take many different forms. Business, political, religious, academic, military, and research and development leaders have different missions, roles, and responsibilities. While there are common elements of leadership in all these categories, each has its distinct characteristics. For example, political leadership typically requires the ability to give excellent speeches. For business leaders, however, this capability is optional. The main difference is that politicians in a democratic society must be elected to succeed, while this is not true for business leaders. That is, political leaders are *elected*, while leaders in the other categories of leadership are *selected*. Therefore, the pressures on political leaders are significantly different from those on leaders in other categories.

Successful leadership in each category is difficult to measure. The suggestion here is to measure success by *results* rather than *style*. This is especially true for business leadership, the category addressed in this work. Business leadership is characterized by *realism* and not *idealism*.

That is not to suggest that good business leadership is irresponsible and ignores social responsibilities. Business leadership must be responsible and accountable to the entire set of stakeholders: the owners, customers, employees, suppliers, and members of the community in which the business operates. So, the results of business leadership must be measured in the context of improving the economic value of these five stakeholder groups. In summary, good business leaders must be *responsible realists*.

Much of the literature on types and styles of leadership defines four different types of leadership. These include:

- autocratic leadership,

- democratic leadership,

- laissez-faire leadership, and

- paternalistic leadership.

These four styles can and do exist within each of the categories of leadership listed above. Each can have various degrees of success depending on the entity's circumstances and the environment. Exclusive of style, qualities, capabilities, skills, and talents required of the leader will differ for each category. This is due to the differences in the overall mission of the leader working in each category.

Aside from the four *styles* of leadership, it's important to note that not all forms of leadership naturally translate into different fields. For example, note the differences in mission and motivation for each leadership field.

- Business leaders create economic value for their stakeholders.

- Political leaders keep citizens safe and create an environment for prosperity.

- Religious leaders serve humanity through spiritual guidance and renewal.

- Academic leaders develop students and provide an environment and curriculum for learning.

- Military leaders defend and protect their country.

- Research and development leaders unlock the mysteries of nature and create things that never were.

Each role is unique and thus requires a unique set of talents and skills.

BUSINESS LEADERSHIP MODEL

To understand and discuss business leadership effectively, it is helpful to consider a model of leadership that includes all aspects and skills associated with leading and managing.

Much of the literature on leadership focuses on the softer aspects of leadership, including emotional intelligence. This is especially true on the various blogs and websites associated with leadership. The leadership model proposed here includes the soft aspects (managing oneself and interpersonal skills) and the more concrete aspects (management skills, strategy, and organizational alignment) that form the management and strategic aspects of defining and leading a business.

The following diagram expresses a useful model for the major components of business leadership:

The *foundation* of good business leadership is the ability to *manage oneself.* Much business literature is devoted to this topic beginning with the seminal article by Peter Drucker (Drucker, 1999). Upon this foundation rests a structure of interpersonal and management skills. Tying this structure together is the overarching ability to develop a strategy and align the workforce to follow this strategy.[3]

---

[3] Key literature that supports this leadership model can be found in several works on leadership (including [Covey, 1989 and 1992], [Collins, 2001], [Porter, 2009], [Schwartz and McCarthy, 2007], [Oncken and Wass, 1999], [Goleman, 2004], and [Zidarić, 2015], among many others).

A NEW BUSINESS LEADERSHIP TOOL

With the information explosion caused by electronic communication, we are inundated with reading materials. Sorting, searching, and screening mechanisms are helpful, but important materials often must be noticed in the barrage of items coming at us. Therefore, the need for "Touchstones" to keep our organizations moving through the ever-changing landscape consistent with our strategic objectives is becoming increasingly important as a tool in managing organizations.

Thus, when the leader is confronted with a challenging situation, they can draw upon this well of learnings to help craft a better direction to address the challenge. *The Touchstones of Leadership* provides a tool to aid in developing leaders at all levels in the organization to become *responsible realists*. It's a guidebook that helps leaders navigate their positions' unique challenges.

> The *foundation* of good business leadership is the ability to *manage oneself.*

Over time, many of us have used certain familiar quotes or sayings to guide the more difficult issues faced by business leaders daily. In this book, I've organized a finite list of forty-five short Touchstones to help business leaders guide themselves, their people, their organization, and their strategy—each organized into one of the four leadership model competency areas.

The goal of this tool is not to *memorize* all forty-five Touchstones but to *internalize* the concepts they represent.

PART 1
Managing Oneself

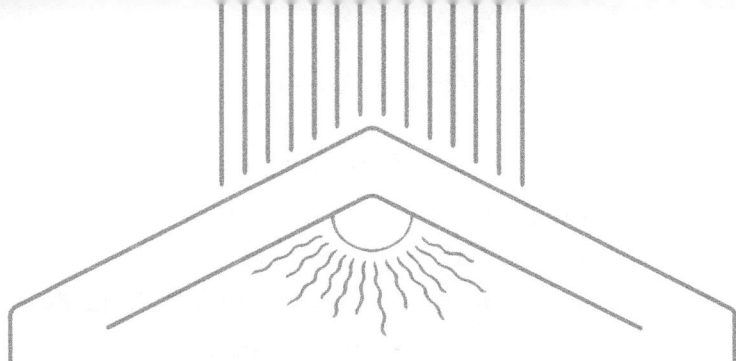

TOUCHSTONE #1

Don't Focus on Things Outside of Your Control

In years of leading different organizations—from R&D to high-volume manufacturing, program management to general management, marketing to business development, and engineering to CEO—I have found that people often get caught up in worrying about things beyond their control.

Will the company be sold? What will happen to me if a new CEO is appointed? Will another part of the world dominate this product? Our competitor is much bigger than we are—will they crush us? And on and on.

While these can be significant concerns, and leaders should be aware of them and have mitigation plans in place, the best thing to do in all cases is to do the best job we can and not worry about what is outside our control. Being overly concerned will reduce productivity, inhibit creativity, increase stress, and lead to a lack of team spirit. This can paralyze an organization. It is up to the leader to get people back on track, ease their concerns, and return the organization to a state of productivity.

In *The Seven Habits of Highly Effective People*, Stephen R. Covey introduces the concept of the "Circle of Concern and the Circle of Influence" (Covey, 1989). The circle of concern encompasses a wide range of items within and outside one's control. Within the circle of concern is a smaller circle, the circle of influence, which contains items we can control, change, or influence in some meaningful way.

The key to the Covey model is to focus on one's circle of influence and work diligently to expand that circle. Often, people don't realize how many things they can influence. A good question to ask yourself is: *In selling or influencing a project or idea, do I take the proper time to prepare my case and frame it in a style most receptive to the decision-makers?* Staying focused on the right things will eliminate the tendency to worry about things beyond one's control and refocus your energy on creating value for the company. This will also provide the satisfaction that you are making a difference.

Furthermore, worrying about things outside your control causes *reactive* rather than *proactive* behavior. It saps your energy. People with visionary behavioral characteristics focus on influencing the organization to change or move in a different direction to achieve the goal, such as winning a new project, streamlining a process, developing a new business relationship, making a convincing customer presentation, and many more. They can't achieve these if they are worried about something out of their control. Such worries inherently cause a lack of self-confidence needed to gain new and more significant accomplishments.

In selling or influencing a project or idea, do I take the proper time to prepare my case and frame it in a style most receptive to the decision-makers?

This is not to suggest we should not be aware of those outside our circle of influence, as they can influence our direction and decision-making. The point is that once the direction and goals are set, good business leaders stay focused and keep their teams focused; poor business leaders do not.

To this point, Bill Gates and Warren Buffett first met at a dinner party hosted by Gates's mother. The dinner guests were asked to identify what led to their success in life. Gates and Buffett gave the same answer: focus (Zitelmann, 2019). Of course, this focus must be directed to the right things that will add value to your business.

Takeaways: Don't Focus on Things Outside Your Control

The Circle of Concern:

- There is a wide range of concerns over which we have little or no control.
- The concerns include the economy and government regulations.
- Focusing on the Circle of Concern causes reactive behavior and saps your energy.

The Circle of Influence:

- This includes concerns we can do something about.
- It also includes things we can directly influence and change.
- It's best to focus efforts on the Circle of Influence and work to expand it.

Additional Points to Remember:

- Giving emotional and mental energy to things outside your control is a waste of time.
- Worry about things you can change.
- Plan for the things you cannot change.
- Avoid rumination by thinking about past or future events in a negative way.
- Focus is a major key to success.

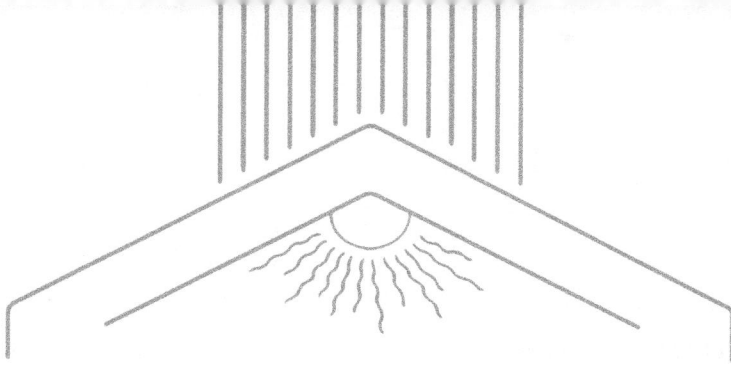

TOUCHSTONE # 2

Never Mistake Activity for Achievement

Have you ever finished a busy workday and wondered if you created anything valuable? Or, when evaluating your team members, have you observed that some work hard and keep long hours but never achieve results? They get stuck in the so-called urgent but not important quadrant of the "Eisenhower Matrix." These situations exemplify the classic case of being consumed with unimportant tasks.

At all levels in a business organization, it is essential to avoid getting bogged down with activities that do not lead to results that create value and improve the business or organization. It's easy to allow routine activities to consume valuable time and sap energy. But it is essential to manage your energy and not just your time. Save everyday tasks for times when your creative juices are low (Schwartz and McCarthy, 2007).

The easy decisions getting to the top of the organization are indicators that activity is being recognized more than results. It implies that the frontline managers are not doing their job but passing the accountability and responsibility upward to the next management level (Oncken and Wass, 1999). It looks like a lot is going on, but in reality, nothing of value is being achieved, and a lot of valuable time is consumed.

Active employees and managers who put in long hours often seem impressive. This impression can last a long time, giving the leader a false sense that they have a productive employee. No one works harder than them, but the job is still not getting done. The critical evaluation, therefore, needs to be based on results and outcomes. So, look for creative ways to measure achievement among your team members.

When I was working at Aerojet, we employed a methodology to develop performance objectives and metrics, which were parsed out and flowed through the entire organization. It used the concept of key result areas (KRAs), which a consulting company developed. This approach involves all levels of leadership. KRAs are first defined in a collaborative process. There are usually five or six KRAs for a company. Two or three objectives for the coming year are set for each KRA. Then, metrics are established for each objective. These measurements are then parsed for each organization in the company. This approach proved very effective and was significant in the turnaround of Aerojet Fine Chemicals, a former subsidiary of Aerojet General Corporation.

Hard workers who don't achieve results are often in the wrong position. For example, a highly qualified but risk-averse person may not do well as the manager of an R&D organization but perform better when moved to the head of a quality assurance organization. This illustrates why leaders must continually measure achievement both on an individual basis and on a corporate basis to optimize the organization.

Takeaways: Never Mistake Activity for Achievement

Stay Focused:

- Don't get bogged down with activities that do not lead to results that strengthen the business.
- Don't permit routine activities to impose on valuable time and sap energy.
- Save routine tasks for times when your creative juices are low.

Manage Your Energy:

- Remember that it's easy to work very hard and accomplish little.
- Don't allow others to place accountability for their tasks on you.
- In evaluating subordinates, ensure results, not efforts, are rated appropriately.

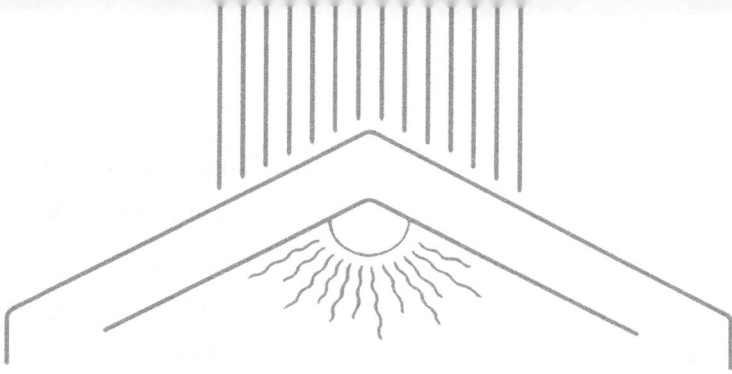

TOUCHSTONE #3

For Minor Matters, Trust Your Mind; for Major Matters, Rely on Your Gut

Minor, in this context, does not mean unimportant. It suggests matters that are more directly addressable and matters the decision-makers can get their arms around more easily because most of the facts are there to be analyzed. On the contrary, significant, or major, matters are ones that are constrained by aspects that are somewhat out of our control, such as the complexity of the situation, time, and lack of data. Insightful gut feeling is typically required in four problematic areas:

- Chaotic | Where an issue is poorly defined

- Crises | When rapid response is required with no time for detailed analysis

- Change | When things are changing so fast that no detailed data exist

- Cryptic | For highly ambiguous issues where the factors are somewhat contradictory

Many of us have been taught that rigorous analysis and the detailed, critical interpretations of those analytical results are essential to dealing with difficult decisions. The difficulty of making significant decisions is that the process possesses an artful component and is more than just a science. The decision-makers and decision influencers must often rely on their experience base to put the incomplete dataset in perspective.

As business leaders, we are often required to assess the situation and decide how to move forward on a schedule incompatible with gathering more data or conducting a more complete analysis. We recognize that an imperfect decision is often better than delaying a decision, as certain critical items need timely attention. Gut feeling or intuitive intelligence is required in these situations. This intuitive intelligence (Bacon, 2015) results from our brain unconsciously synthesizing information and experiences to arrive at different and less obvious solutions.

Intuitive intelligence is a nonlinear and essential skill for success in the new economy driven by constant disruption and chaos. It can be defined as the combination of four abilities:

- the ability to see the whole picture and put it in context

- the ability to hold conflicting thoughts simultaneously

- the ability to empathize when listening

- the ability to use influence as a leadership tool

These abilities allow one to see the whole picture and decide quickly on the direction to achieve the objective. Moreover, neuroscience studies estimate that the brain has a fantastic memory capacity with estimates in the petabyte range (i.e., the capacity of the entire World Wide Web). Beyond capacity, the unconscious processing speed has been estimated at over five trillion operations per second, and cellular biologists estimate that 95 percent of our actions, emotions, and behaviors are based on processing by the subconscious mind (Eksteen, 2019).

Furthermore, when new information is presented, the brain determines how this information might fit with other stored information. It turns out that the subconscious mind connects with this stored information in unique ways that trigger new thinking and ideas. This is often referenced as intelligent memory, intuition, or gut feeling (Gordon and Berger, 2003).

Solving high-level organizational problems often requires a gut feeling since there is usually no concrete information to support the solution. When I was appointed president of Fine Chemicals Company, a subsidiary of Aerojet, the business was in significant financial distress. It was burning cash quickly, the loan instrument was fully drawn, and new business was languishing.

During the first few weeks on the job, I interviewed many of the managers and employees, and it became evident that the only way to turn things around was to embark on a significant cost-reduction exercise to balance the costs with the expected revenue generation. The organization was overstaffed for its current revenue, requiring a 40 percent reduction in employees from 250 to 150 to align costs.

This is where gut feeling came into play. Many said it was impossible to run the business as configured with 40 percent fewer employees. Experience and gut feeling, however, provided the insight that with the proper reorganization and convincing the team that this must and could be done, the team could make this work. It took a gut feeling and experience to convince the team that there was inefficiency in the operation for the current level of business and that this needed to be corrected.

Furthermore, as the business level grew, we could restaff the organization. To motivate those remaining, it was essential to reduce the management structure and hourly staff by 40 percent, which we did. There was some resistance during the reorganization process. The most significant, among a few managers, was the reduction in the workforce. Our manufacturing manager was so upset that the manager sent a letter to me and the operations vice president that if we undertook this 40 percent reduction-in-force, we would create a safety problem in the manufacturing operation.

Again, collaboration among the senior team and gut feeling convinced me that this reorganization did not increase our risk in safety to personnel, facilities, or products. Because of these actions, the subsidiary began to turn a profit and eventually grow. This business flourished and maintained a strong and profitable growth profile.

Hiring personnel is another area requiring a gut feeling. It is one of a leader's most important actions. Successful hiring requires a gut feeling based on our experiences. One must recognize the analytical part of the hiring process and collect data, especially from references, but to get the right fit requires intuition.

This is because three questions must be satisfied to hire success-fully: *Is the candidate technically qualified? Does the candidate have high integrity? Will the candidate fit the culture of the organization?* Assessing this last requirement relies on a good gut feeling by the hiring leader and others participating in the hiring process.

Takeaways: For Minor Matters, Trust Your Mind; for Major Matters, Rely on Your Gut

Three Constraints on Significant Decisions:

- The complexity of the situation.
- Time.
- Lack of data.

Effective Decision-Making Is an Art:

- Making major decisions is a process that has an artful component.
- Analysis is necessary but insufficient.
- Decision-makers must rely on their experience to put incomplete data in perspective.
- Gut feeling is needed when there is a crisis, chaos, change, or a cryptic situation.
- Intuitive intelligence is the result of our brain unconsciously synthesizing info and experiences to arrive at different and less obvious solutions.
- An imperfect decision is sometimes better than delaying a decision because certain critical items need timely attention.

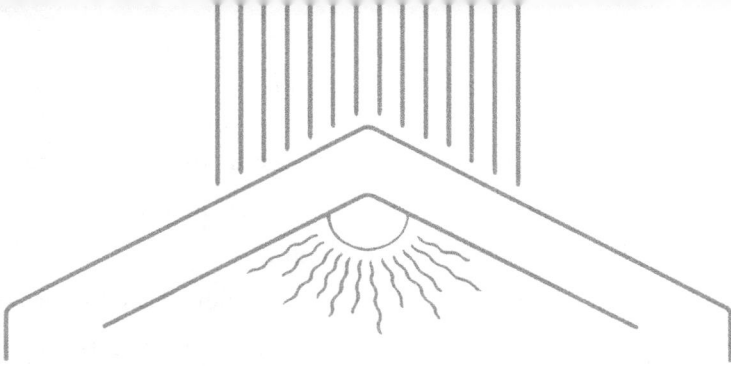

TOUCHSTONE # 4

Consider Using the Seventy-Two-Hour Rule When Faced with a Major Surprise

As a business progresses, surprises often have negative effects on the company. These can take many different forms. Product test failures, unexplainable manufacturing difficulties, customer complaints, and regulatory issues can all arise.

When these situations occur, it is often best to *investigate* before *reacting*. Very often, initial reports during a crisis need to be corrected. It usually takes seventy-two hours to grasp the essence of the problem and put a plan in place to deal with the issue. This number is not scientifically based, but based on experience, seventy-two hours is a good rule of thumb.

In this era of electronic communication, many want instant answers and instant decisions. But it is not helpful to make quick responses and take serious action on unexpected surprises. A short investigative period, settling the situation, and "sleeping" on the data often pay off one-hundred-fold. Of course, there are exceptions, such as life-threatening or other dangerous situations where immediate action is necessary and warranted. The key in these situations is to separate the response from the stimulus. This is often necessary to ensure the surprise is genuinely a problem.

I recall one incident during a product development program for the military. It was a high-visibility program, and there was a component test failure of an explosive device. Unfortunately, it was immediately reported to the entire chain of command before any cause analysis was performed. Forty or fifty military and civilian personnel of the Department of Defense descended upon us under the assumption that the design failed.

After many days of discussion and meetings, speculations of the cause resulted in many hours of work and debate. It turned out there was a simple test set-up error, which could have been discovered in a few hours of problem-solving once all the information was assembled. Instead, a lot of misinformation circled the halls of the Pentagon, and a lot of unnecessary work was done. If we had waited seventy-two hours before reporting this anomaly, we could have also reported the cause. This benign failure would have been easily rectified.

Personnel matters are often very tricky issues to handle. Timing is critical, and a leader must often "bag the schedule" to address the issue. Unlike good wine, personnel matters typically do not get better with age. Thus, the seventy-two-hour rule may be significantly shortened when handling these specific issues.

Takeaways: Consider Using the Seventy-Two-Hour Rule When Faced with a Major Surprise

Don't Overreact:

- Urgent issues typically take seventy-two hours to grasp.
- Ensure it is truly a problem.
- Initial reports are often wrong.
- Exceptions to the rule include matters of immediate material consequence.

Making Wise Decisions:

- It's best to get several sides of the issue before taking an irreversible position.
- Separate the response from the stimulus.
- The seventy-two-hour rule may often have to be shortened regarding personnel and environment, health, and safety issues.

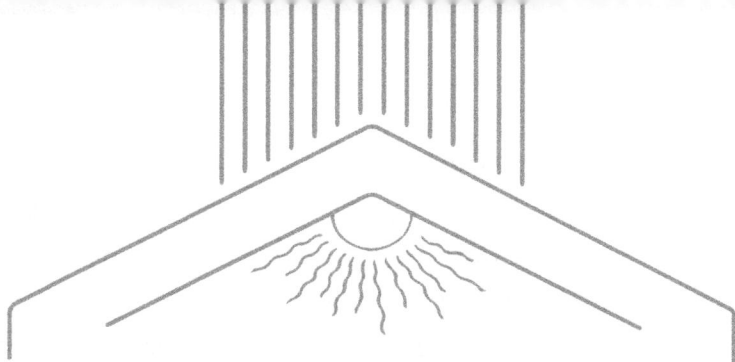

TOUCHSTONE #5

Focus on Relationships and Results, Not Activities and Time-Saving

Leaders at all levels in a business organization must constantly consider the long-term aspects of their decisions and actions.

To be successful in the long term requires relationships with colleagues, external customers, internal customers, suppliers, bosses, subordinates, owners, and those in the community. This includes both our global business community and the local community in which we operate. Developing solid relationships through engendering trust and mutual respect allows us to challenge one another without creating impediments and destroying collaboration. This is the only way we can get the best result when trying to solve a problem, develop a business plan, allocate capital, or develop a new strategic direction. This applies on the shop floor as well as in the board room. These relationships will drive the quality of the results the business will achieve.

Strong relationships will deter groupthink. Groupthink (Janis, 1982) is one of the most detrimental situations in an organization. It is a social phenomenon where the desire of individuals for harmony overrides the desire for critical thinking. Groupthink often arises because relationships between individuals are weak, and the fear of being open among the group suppresses the debate required to reach the best outcome. This is especially detrimental during strategic planning, launching a new venture, making critical decisions on capital planning, or solving a personnel problem.

In team structures, we need to be able to challenge one another to achieve high-quality results. This requires trust and the right chemistry. Furthermore, we must not create problems that don't exist. That is, don't "overthink." Risks must be taken to grow, both personally and in business. The fear of office politics must be avoided, and we must never make differences personal. Much of this can be avoided through solid personal relationships where we can mutually define objective metrics and focus on the quality of objectives, not their quantity.

> Groupthink is one of the most detrimental situations in an organization.

Working on developing strong relationships is critical to achieving results. It takes time to identify and determine the suitable activities to pursue. Choosing the right path to follow is essential for the health and growth of the business. To make this choice, we must be able to unleash the full power of the organization. Trust and mutual respect are necessary for us to debate the various options to an extent that will enable the highest-quality result. Trust reduces the need for excessive bureaucracy in an organization. Activities move much faster, and people buy into the results. Motivation is also high when there is a feeling of trust throughout the organization, and personal relationships remain strong.

Research shows that employees desire purpose in their lives and that 70 percent of them have stated that their sense of purpose is primarily defined by their work (Dhingra et al., 2021). While most executives have a strong sense of purpose in their day-to-day work, many frontline managers and workers do not feel their daily work provides an adequate sense of purpose. This research further reveals that one of the primary reasons for this gap between executives and frontline workers is the lack of upper management's sharing of the company's overarching purpose and strategic plan with all employees.

Sharing the "big picture" will improve relationships, build trust, and help devote a sense of purpose to day-to-day work. Getting to know employees and empathizing with their concerns will also help develop the necessary relationships. Further, how to build relationships is discussed in Part 2, Interpersonal Skills.

Takeaways: Focus on Relationships and Results, Not Activities and Time-Saving

Build Strong Relationships:

- Success in the long term requires relationships with colleagues, internal customers, bosses, subordinates, external customers, suppliers, owners, and those in our community. Strong relationships engender trust and mutual respect.
- Don't "groupthink." Develop strong relationships so that we can challenge one another without destroying the relationship. Don't let the desire for harmony override the urge for critical thinking.
- Don't fear office politics and avoid making differences personal.

Communicate Well:

- Don't create problems that don't exist. Don't "overthink." Risks must be taken to grow, both personally and in the business.
- Key metrics: measure quality versus quantity.
- Take the time and effort to identify the "right" activities to pursue.
- Share the company's "big picture" throughout the organization.

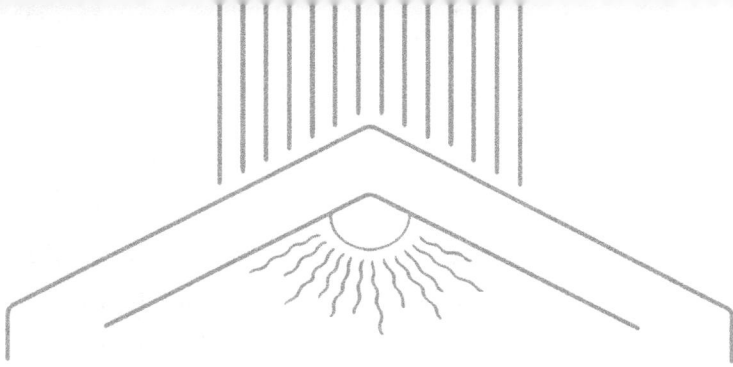

T O U C H S T O N E # 6

Let Your Principles, Not Circumstances, Guide Your Behavior

In *Principle-Centered Leadership* (Covey, 1992), Stephen Covey makes a significant point about the difference between principles and values.

Covey notes that *principles* are external qualities akin to laws of nature, apparently inevitable phenomena observable in human society, while *values* are beliefs an organization holds. Values help formulate the strategic direction of a business and become the foundation of an operating plan. Principles are immutable laws; values may morph as business and technology advance.

Most of us can agree on the following principles to guide a business operation (Covey, 1992):

FAIRNESS	PATIENCE	HONESTY
KINDNESS	INTEGRITY	QUALITY
DIGNITY	CHARITY	SERVICE

If internalized by the organization, these principles will drive trust and respect. These principles will not change, like the laws of nature. Covey refers to them as the territories, while values are the maps. Values must be aligned with these principles to guide the organization effectively. Sometimes, a value and a principle may be identical. For example, many companies identify quality as a value.

Value statements have a place to provide guidance, but values must be aligned with the principles stated above and internalized by the business members. Many companies have good value statements that align with our discussed principles. For example, Enron had the following displayed as values in their lobby:

- integrity

- communication

- respect

- excellence

But since some of Enron's executives were jailed and the company went bankrupt because of fraud, these clearly were not Enron's *actual* values. Behaviors and skills exhibited and valued by employees are the actual values of any company. We can understand the actual values by examining who gets hired, promoted, and let go.

Principles are immutable laws; values may morph as business and technology advance.

The message here is that as a leader, you may run into difficult or uncomfortable circumstances where there will be pressure to make a critical decision that needs to be clear-cut. When this happens, make sure that the principles mentioned above guide your response, not the situation's circumstances. It is your choice how to respond to difficult circumstances.

Takeaways: Let Your Principles, Not Circumstances, Guide Your Behavior

Stick to Your Principles:

- Principles are qualities akin to the laws of nature and are observable phenomena.
- The fundamental principles to guide a business include fairness, kindness, dignity, patience, integrity, charity, honesty, quality, and service.
- In a difficult situation, don't opt for a quick solution that is not aligned with your principles.

Know Your Values:

- Values are important beliefs held by a culture.
- Values must be aligned with principles.
- Correct principles and values will drive trust and respect.
- Consistency is essential.
- Remember that "it begins with me."

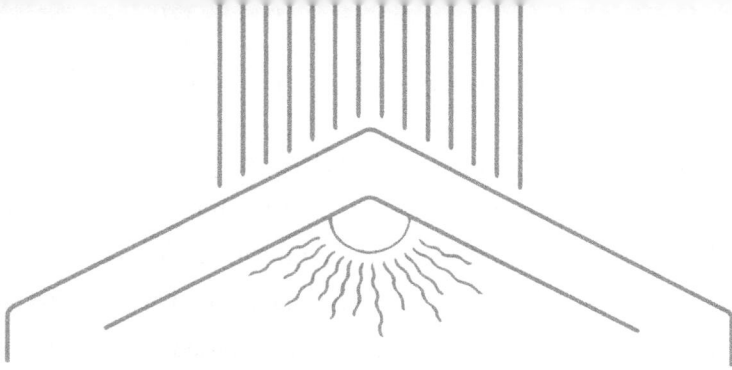

TOUCHSTONE #7

When You Are Out Selling, Never Discuss Religion or Politics

Religious beliefs and political preferences are not germane to almost every business transaction, and discussing these beliefs will not add value to any business setting.

Fundamentally, these two topics, politics and religion, can initiate passionate responses when broached, often causing serious arguments that have nothing to do with the business matter. During such discussions, there is often a sudden emotional outburst, leaving you to say to yourself, "What caused that?"

Why other topics do not elicit such explosive and divisive reactions? We are never warned about discussing sports, music, cars, movies, photography, or flying airplanes. People can be very passionate about these subjects, too, but for some reason, these topics tend not to be as sensitive even when we disagree with one another on them (Green, 2018).

Politics and religion are very sensitive because they are extremely personal and unique for everyone. As we experience life, we form views and beliefs that evolve and deal with the accumulation of positive and negative events in our lives. Our positions on these topics tend to become deeply entrenched. Often, specific issues associated with religion or politics are underpinned by moral conviction (Skitka, 2010; 2021). Topics underpinned by moral conviction are much more a part of our internal fabric than topics associated with preferences, taste, and experience. Challenging positions based on moral conviction can trigger feelings of threat and anxiety and become divisive.

Thus, it is best if you don't discuss your religious beliefs or your thoughts about other religious beliefs while in the presence of customers (or at work, for that matter). This doesn't mean you should hide your religion or shouldn't be proud of it, but keep in mind it is a personal topic that can cause people to react very emotionally. When you are out selling, your job is to build relationships and not destroy trust by trying to prove your worldview is correct. Most customers or clients don't want to hear you disagree with their religious beliefs or that you believe your religion is the one everyone should believe (Greer, 2015).

> Religious beliefs and political preferences are not germane to almost every business transaction, and discussing these beliefs will not add value to any business setting.

People are also very sensitive about their political beliefs; therefore, you should avoid getting into lengthy political conversations. While you may feel strongly about your party or have negative views about the opposition, you should not try to win your customers (or coworkers) over to your side. It is unlikely to happen anyway and will cause hard feelings between you and them.

Listen politely and empathetically if a customer or coworker forces the conversation toward these topics. Avoid commenting either positively or negatively. Even if you agree with the argument, it is best not to comment. The trick is to graciously work your way back to the business at hand or to another topic.

Takeaways: When You Are Out Selling, Never Discuss Religion or Politics

Remember:

- Topics such as sports, music, cars, and movies are less sensitive than politics and religion.
- Religious and political beliefs are underpinned by moral conviction.
  - They are developed over our entire life.
  - They are based on successes and failures.
  - People inherently feel that beliefs tied to moral convictions should apply to everyone, as compared with matters of taste or preference.
- Customers don't want to hear you disagree with their firmly held political and religious beliefs.
- This doesn't mean you should hide your religion or not be proud of it.
  - Don't promote it.
  - Don't proselytize.
  - Don't criticize other religions or political parties.
- After you know someone well, you can soften these guidelines a bit (but only a little).

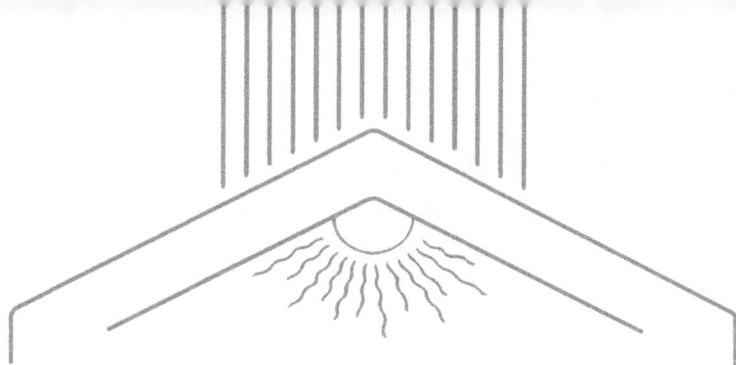

TOUCHSTONE # 8

Never Pursue Glory; Pursue Excellence

It is natural for people to desire recognition for the results they produce, but it is not wise to have the end goal as recognition or glory.

Focusing on the recognition aspect of a project or decision can remove the focus necessary for a successful result, especially in the longer term. It will encourage cutting corners and an attempt to accelerate the task to achieve "success" sooner without the permanence necessary to be truly successful. Seeking glory will only distort the quality of the outcome by emphasizing short-term over long-term results.

Furthermore, people will easily see through the immediate actions of those who seek only glory and recognize their true motivations. Of course, this will immediately destroy credibility and lead to a complete loss of trust and respect within the organization. You often find these "glory seekers" when you recruit someone for a senior position who looks at the job as merely a stepping stone to the next promotion. They are not motivated to contribute significantly to the business and start looking for the next position almost immediately after they are hired.

It isn't always easy to spot "glory seekers" during the recruiting process. I recall one instance where we recruited a new vice president of manufacturing operations. The selected candidate had an excellent résumé and credible references. He managed upward very well, his presentations to the Board of Directors were exceptional, and the manufacturing team initially received him well. After a few months, however, there were no tangible results of his direct efforts. Morale within his organization waned, and he took credit for all the positive things happening and pointed the finger at other organizations for the negative occurrences. As a result, we had to separate within a year, and the company lost considerable time and opportunities.

> It is natural for people to desire recognition for the results they produce, but it is not wise to have the end goal as recognition or glory.

Business leaders must develop the ability to focus on excellence as they guide their businesses. Encouraging and even demanding excellence from all personnel and in all major business processes will set the tone for a high-performance workplace. This starts with demanding excellence from oneself. A leader who does not exhibit this characteristic will not be able to engender a penchant for excellence within the organization's culture. Pursuing excellence may be harder, but it will yield more permanent results. The recognition or glory will come because of the endurable success.

As you pursue excellence, the concept of being a winner (Luntz, 2011) is helpful. In this sense, winning is associated with creating actual value that will be recognized by all stakeholders but especially by the customer community. Customers want to place their business with successful companies or winners. Winning is also critical to enhance the business and continue to boost the workforce's morale. Furthermore, winners are characterized as people who want to *do* something, not *be* something.

We need people with a winning mentality at every level in the organization.

Takeaways: Never Pursue Glory; Pursue Excellence

People Want Recognition:

- It's natural for people to desire recognition for their results.
- The end objective should not be glory.
- Glory-seeking reduces focus on the true objective.
- "Corner-cutting" and unnecessary compromises often occur.
- People will see your true motivations.

Excellence Is Necessary:

- Excellence produces better and more permanent results.
- Excellence will lead to endurable success, which will lead to glory coming naturally.
- Winners want to *do* something, not *be* something.

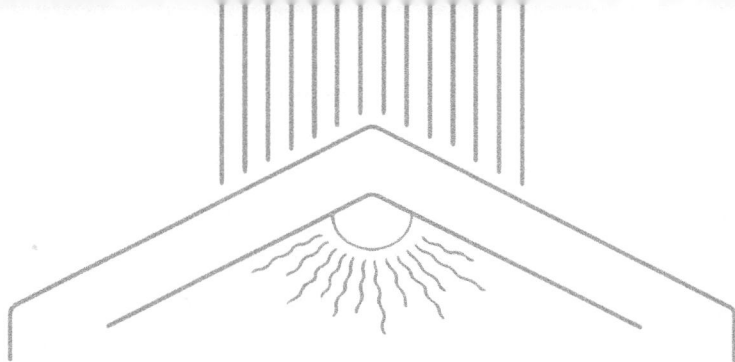

TOUCHSTONE # 9

Procrastinators Are the Leaders of Tomorrow

The results of decision-making and subsequent action are clear measures of how leaders perform. The timing of these decisions and actions will nearly always affect the quality of the results that occur from these decisions and actions.

Procrastinators are paralyzed by their indecision to act and fail to complete tasks on time. There is a clear distinction between one who constantly puts off deciding and a good leader who waits until it is absolutely necessary to make a decision. Timing is everything in decision-making, and making a decision out of convenience versus waiting for appropriate information is an important distinction.

Patience is essential. We have seen leaders who want to make the decision to get the problem behind them, but this is irresponsible leadership. Waiting too long is also irresponsible. So, there is a fine line between good decision-makers and traditional procrastinators.

Research has been conducted (Chu, Chun, and Choi, 2005) on so-called "active" procrastinators. These are people who like to work under time pressure. This is not what we mean here. Good decision-makers have a sense of timing. They understand the situation so that they can get the most data before deciding without sacrificing the need to make the decision in a timely enough manner to have the maximum impact on the outcome.

So, there is a fine line between good decision-makers and traditional procrastinators.

Excellent leaders have a unique sense of timing that comes from their experience in the industry and market, experience with and knowledge of their employees, and a deep understanding of the situation at hand.

Winning leaders are excellent at prioritizing high-value activities as most important and do not wait for the so-called perfect time to get things done (Ferrante, 2018). Very often, key decisions must be made at the right time, and a successful leader will not procrastinate because the decision is difficult. Winning leaders possess the following characteristics:

- a drive for success and making timely decisions to keep you in the lead

- the ability to address challenges head-on and be proactive on complex matters

- total commitment and the motivation to act

Fear of failure can create paralysis in decision-making. This can be overcome by good planning. If decision A fails, is there a backup plan B that will allow the business to move forward? Very often, we learn a lot from early failures. Delaying decisions will cause such failures to happen much later in the project when there is less time to introduce a backup plan.

Takeaways: Procrastinators Are the Leaders of Tomorrow

Timing and Practice Are Important:

- There is a clear distinction between one who constantly puts off a decision versus one who waits until necessary to decide.
- Deciding just to get it behind you is irresponsible.
- Putting it off too long is also irresponsible.
- Excellent leaders have a special sense of timing. This comes from (a) experience in the industry, (b) experience and knowledge of the employees, and (c) deep understanding of the situation.

Overcome Your Fears and Win:

- Fear of failure can create paralysis in making decisions.
- Overcome by good planning and always having a backup plan.
- Winning leaders are excellent at prioritizing high-value activities.
- Winners drive for success and remember that timely decisions keep them in the lead.
- Winners address challenges head-on and are proactive on difficult, important matters.
- Winners are completely committed and motivated to act.

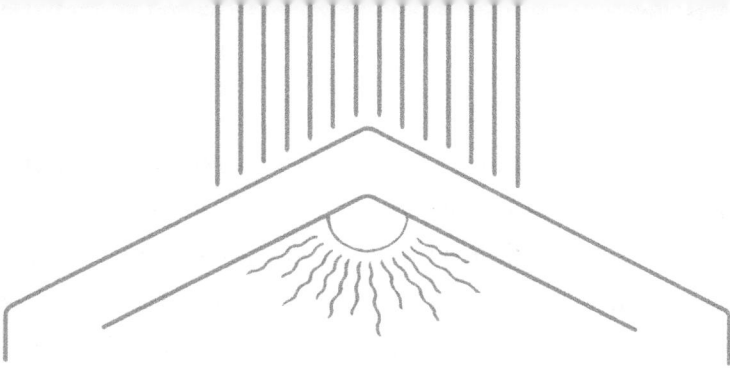

TOUCHSTONE #10

Sometimes You Must Take a Step Back to Take Two Steps Forward

Persistence is essential for success. Of course, we must always be careful that persistence focuses on the desired result, not the activity. It is too easy to become enamored with the process and diverge from where we want to go.

We all try to keep pressing forward on our current path, whether our careers, our current project, or building a relationship. As we pursue these, however, we may realize we are on the wrong path. When this suspicion arises, it is often advantageous to take a step back and review the overall landscape and strategy of what got us to where we are. There may be a different off-ramp we should take to get us to a new path. We may see a new strategy. We may modify the current strategy based on some further information.

You may be down the path a good distance when you detect it is wrong, and a disaster may be coming. Don't panic. Accept the harsh reality that your current path—no matter how much you are in love with it—will not get you there. Take a step back and reevaluate the situation. There is a way to recover in most cases. Don't give up and keep moving forward.

A classic example of stepping back and off the wrong path is the making of the movie *Toy Story 2*. As Disney pushed Pixar for a difficult schedule for theatrical release, the leadership at Pixar, especially Lasseter, was unhappy with the film's quality. Pixar decided they could not allow the film to be released in its existing state and completely redeveloped its plot. As we know now, it became a rousing success, but there was a time when it was likely to fail without some significant course corrections.

Takeaways: Sometimes You Must Take a Step Back to Take Two Steps Forward

Move Forward with Objectives:

- That said, we may find (or suspect) that we are on the wrong path.
- If this is the case, stopping and taking a step back is advantageous.
- Review the overall landscape and strategy.
- There may be a new or modified path forward.

If You're on the Wrong Path:

- Don't panic.
- Review the situation and strategy.
- Remember there is most often a way to recover.
- Be persistent and focus on results.
- Be resilient in tough times.
- Accept harsh realities.
- Find meaning in setbacks.
- Improvise.

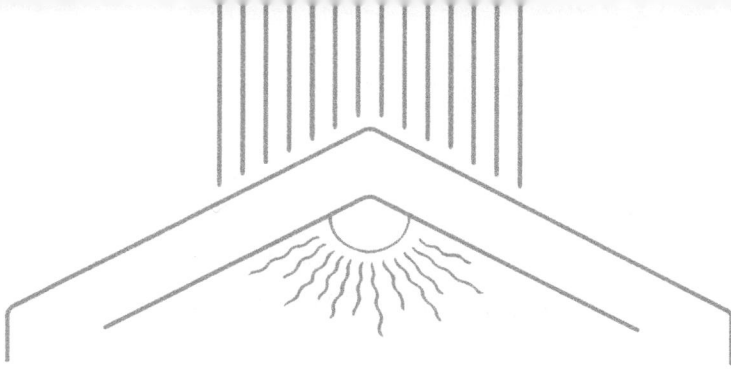

TOUCHSTONE #11

Those Who Dare to Teach Never Cease to Learn

As you quietly ponder and develop your business strategy and associated action plan, think seriously about how you will communicate the plan to your team. The best way to learn and develop a complex subject is to teach it.

Your team expects you to teach them what you know. The teaching is often quite informal. It can be by example rather than direct instruction. You must be aware that you are always teaching, whether you like it or not, and the example can be good or bad.

Learning can be improved greatly when you are planning to teach a subject. When you are preparing to teach, your mind is more likely to consider possible questions that may come up. In addition, preparing to teach can motivate you to research the topic more extensively, beyond the planned material. This can give you a deeper understanding of the subject and provide the necessary context for the material you will be teaching.

> The best way to learn and develop a complex subject is to teach it.

Also, preparing to teach helps you learn about who your team is and how to adapt to the team's natural learning styles. You will generate new methods to help your team understand the subject or project. Stephen Covey (Covey, 1989) conveys this principle in his writings and his teachings.

I was fortunate in the late 1980s to hear from him directly in a small group. In 1988, I reported to the president of a subsidiary of Aerojet General Corporation. He had been associated with the teachings of Covey and brought Dr. Covey to meet with him and his direct staff for a day and for Dr. Covey to teach us the *Seven Habits of Highly Effective People*. Dr. Covey hadn't achieved worldwide notoriety yet, and it was amazing to have the personal attention of this distinguished teacher and expert.

One of the main themes of his discussions with us was this aspect of teaching a subject to learn it better. At the end of the session, the assignment was for each of us to take the material we learned, schedule a session with our respective staff, and teach this material to them in an all-day session. Since then, it also became clear to me that teams *expect* us to share our knowledge, philosophy, and experiences with them. Having a teaching mindset facilitates the achievement of those expectations.

Takeaways: Those Who Dare to Teach Never Cease to Learn

Teach Your Team:

- Your team expects you to teach them what you know.

- Be aware you are always teaching, albeit good or bad.

- Learning is enhanced when you know you are teaching.

Preparing to Teach:

- Allows the mind to anticipate questions.

- Motivates one to research deeper into the topic.

- Allows you to understand your team's (or students') natural learning styles.

- Helps you learn who they truly are.

- Motivates you to develop new methods to help them learn.

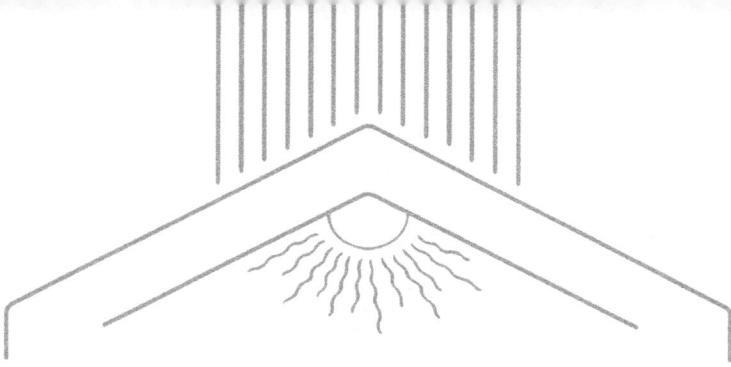

TOUCHSTONE #12

Imagination Is More Important Than Knowledge

Knowledge is constrained by what is currently understood and limited by the body of works that exist. Yes, that body of knowledge will grow in the future, but that growth is driven by those who push the boundaries and experiment with new things that have yet to be envisioned. This is where imagination comes into play. Imagination is the ability of the human mind to see things that don't exist today but could.

This Touchstone is one of Albert Einstein's most famous quotations. In business, we find that imagination occurs at all levels within the organization, and when it does, that business will flourish. Imagination applies not only to the high-level vision and strategy of the company but also to back-office processes, employee benefit packages, and every step through product development and manufacturing. Imagination is especially important in marketing and in developing new businesses.

To put this into perspective, let us review the common definitions:

- *Knowledge*: The facts, information, and skills acquired by a person through experience or education; the theoretical or practical understanding of a subject.

- *Imagination*: The faculty or action of forming new ideas, images, or concepts of external objects not present to the senses.

- *Curiosity*: A strong desire to know or learn something.

- *Creativity*: The ability to make or bring into existence something new.

- *Innovation*: Executing an idea that addresses a specific challenge and achieves value for the company and the customer.

In developing truly new things, be they products, services, business processes, or much more, we begin with imagination. The process of imagining something triggers our curiosity to explore whether this new thing is possible. So, we seek knowledge, whether it is captured by previous learnings or whether we need to research the relevant knowledge base or consult with mentors or experts in the field. Combining imagination, curiosity, and knowledge in a circular fashion leads to creativity. As the creative ideas are fleshed out, the result is innovation.

> Imagination is the ability of the human mind to see things that don't exist today but could.

Research using network science shows that thinking in a creative, or more imaginative, fashion is characterized by connecting ideas or concepts that are further and further apart (Beaty and Kenett, 2020).

For example, connecting the word *box* to a container is much closer than connecting the word *box* to a costume (cut up the box and wear it). The more distant the connection is, the more imaginative it is.

Pixar, the creator of animated feature movies, looks at creativity in a collective way (Catmull, 2008). They firmly state that creativity is a product of several talented people effectively working together to solve problems. Pixar gives each person creative ownership of even the smallest task. Even the design of their building is structured to facilitate informal communications. They give courses that provide tools to stimulate the imagination.

I had questioned whether creativity could be learned until my visit to Pixar. As a member of the UC Davis External Research Advisory Board (ERAB), I met the dean of Pixar University, Pixar's internal learning center. One of ERAB's meetings was held at the Pixar location, and we got to sample some of the training exercises Pixar used to teach creativity. This experience, combined with many discussions during that visit, made me a believer that creativity, indeed, can be learned.

I subsequently discovered that my alma mater, Drexel University, provides a master's program in Creativity and Innovation. Since an organization's creativity is an important factor for success, leaders should consider creativity training as part of their employee development program.

Takeaways: Imagination Is More Important Than Knowledge

- Knowledge concerns what is currently understood.
- Imagination focuses on things that never were but could be, and new ideas start with imagination.
- Imagination leads to curiosity, which spurs a desire for knowledge.
- Combining imagination, curiosity, and knowledge leads to creativity, which results in innovation.

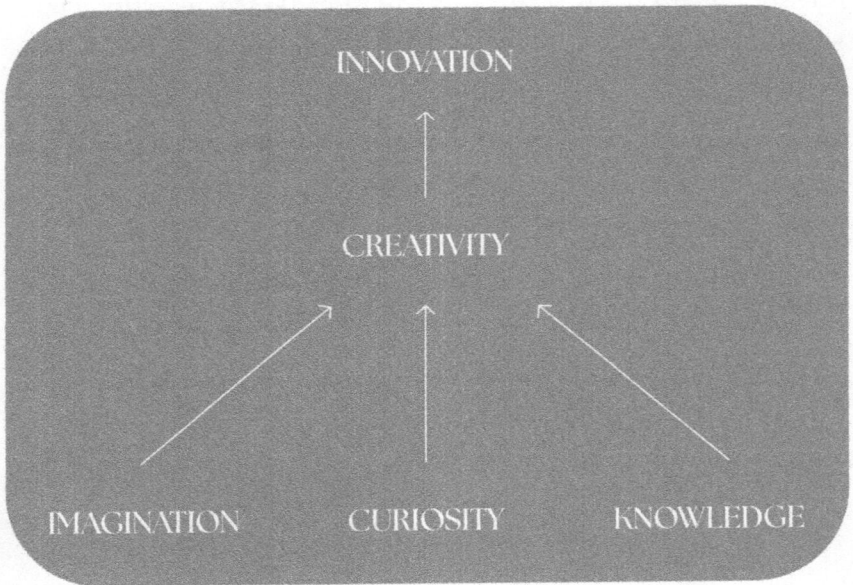

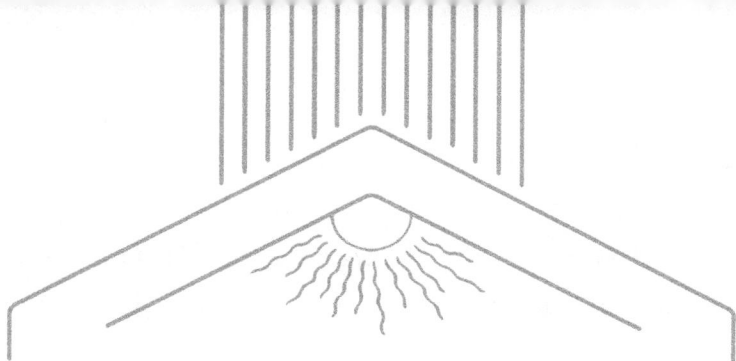

TOUCHSTONE #13

Managing Is Doing Things Right; Leading Is Doing the Right Things

This well-known statement is a great guideline to describe the difference in our overriding responsibilities when operating as managers compared with when we are operating as leaders.

We often hear discussions where management and leadership are treated as two separate things. In reality, a spectrum or continuum of situations combines managing and leading. Most people in the business world do *both* each day, often simultaneously. On some days, it may be more managing and less leading; on other days, it may be just the opposite. So, regardless of position, we must do both, especially in entrepreneurial businesses. Even highly charismatic leaders require an appreciation of, as well as respect for, the importance of managing and need to make sure the execution part of their strategy and vision is covered in an excellent manner.

This interplay between leadership and management gets back to the observation that some people can work very, very hard and not accomplish the desired results. Often, they are working on the wrong things because the strategy's objectives have not been clearly defined.

So, the leadership function is where everything about a business begins. The leadership team must communicate the strategy, define objectives, set priorities, and motivate the organization. Too many top leaders in a company want the team to dive right in and start producing results before there is a proper understanding and, perhaps more importantly, a buy-in by those expected to produce the results. Buy-in throughout the organization is essential to the success of the strategy. Without it, no matter how good the strategy, it will likely fail. As the business world is changing more rapidly than ever, leading the business changes necessary to keep relevant and ahead of the competition is a critical part of the leader's job in defining strategy.

> The best strategy in the world is worthless without good, solid execution.

Management skills and experience are needed to carry out the execution aspects of the strategy by defining near-term actions necessary to achieve long-term strategic goals. This starts with taking each strategic objective and developing a tactical plan that lays out the path for execution. Managing also requires assigning resources to execute the plan, measuring the results achieved, and adjusting the plan as necessary. The best strategy in the world is worthless without good, solid execution (Bamforth, 2020).

There are four keys (Buckingham and Coffman, 1999) that managers, as well as leaders, need to use in running their businesses:

- *Personnel selection*: Select for talent, not only experience, intelligence, or determination.

- *Defining expectations*: Define outcomes, not the process or steps.

- *Provide motivation*: Focus on their strengths, not weaknesses.

- *Personnel development*: Find the right fit, not just the next promotion.

Buckingham and Coffman emphasize these four points, often contrary to many companies' policies. Hence, there is a need for change in leadership.

Takeaways: Managing Is Doing Things Right; Leading Is Doing the Right Things

Lead and Manage:

- Regardless of position, we must do both by managing and leading simultaneously.
- Leadership: Define strategy, set priorities, define objectives, and motivate self and others.
    - To succeed, we must identify the right path.
    - Objectives to achieve the desired results are critical.
- Management: Develop plans, identify best approaches, assign resources, measure results, and adjust as necessary.
- We cannot divert our resources to do the "cool" things.
- Efficiency for the sake of efficiency will lead to failure.
- Buy-in from the team is essential.
- Leadership and management skills are necessary to gain the trust and respect required to achieve buy-in.

Four Keys of Leadership and Management by Buckingham and Coffman:

- Select for talent.
- Define the proper outcomes.
- Focus on strengths.
- Find the right fit.

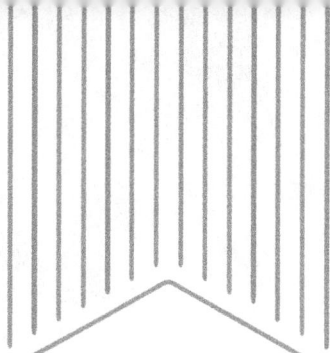

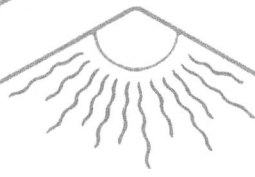

PART 2
Interpersonal Skills

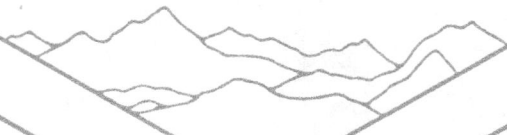

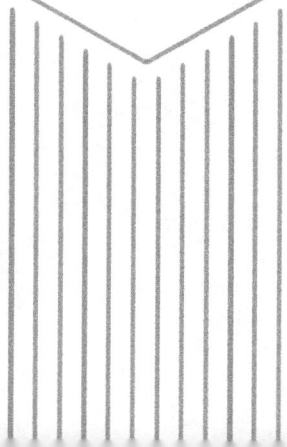

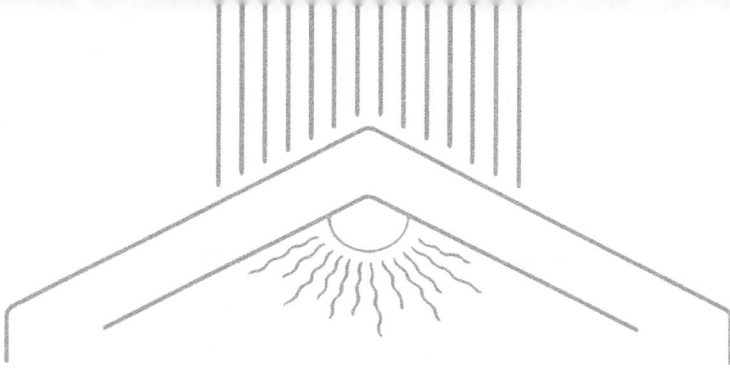

TOUCHSTONE #14

Treat Employees as You Would Want Them to Treat Customers

Why don't people believe CEOs and other business leaders when they say, "People are our most important asset"? Have you ever heard a CEO state the opposite or allude to some other aspect of the company being more important? Furthermore, the CEOs I know genuinely believe this. But often, they are accused of not being sincere when they state this belief.

The reason for this is that CEOs whose sincerity is questioned have yet to instill trust and respect throughout their organizations. As *The Seven Habits of Highly Effective People* (Covey, 1989) pointed out, treating employees as customers is an excellent way to engender this trust.

First, it is essential to recognize that employees provide a significant competitive advantage for the company. Employees are true differentiators when it comes to competing. To grow and maintain this differentiation requires a workforce with high morale and motivation. This requires leaders to develop trust and respect with all workforce members. This is best done by asking for and respecting the ideas of all team members. Also, it is necessary to respect their concerns and needs while ensuring compensation is fair and consistent with the value created in each job.

People become motivated when they know you care about them. They will go the extra mile to make the company a success. So, leaders need to get to know their people. Knowing what makes them unique and their goals will show them you care. People also want the right tools and training to do their job. They also want to know that the company has a strategy to make the company win and that the employees will win along the journey (Kraus, 2017).

> CEOs whose sincerity is questioned have yet to instill trust and respect throughout their organizations.

My father gave me excellent advice when I moved into a general management position and became responsible for R&D, engineering, and manufacturing. He worked for most of his life in a factory that manufactured grinding wheels. When I first told him I was also responsible for manufacturing, he said, "Why don't you go down on the manufacturing floor and ask the operators for suggestions and ideas on how to manufacture the new products being designed?"

He said that industrial engineers would often come to the floor in his plant with their stopwatches and clipboards to figure out how to improve the products or increase productivity. He said, "All they had to do was ask us, but they never did." In those days (1950s and 1960s), manufacturing workers typically didn't offer unsolicited advice to engineers because they were often ignored, and the workers felt the managers and engineers looked down upon them.

I did just what my father suggested, and it was a resounding success. From that point on, there were many informal meetings between the engineers and production workers that improved the manufacturability of the products, reduced costs, and improved the morale of the entire workforce.

Maintaining high employee morale is essential to high performance in your company. In-depth research (Amabile and Kramer, 2011) studied the work lives of more than one thousand American adults and demonstrated that of all the factors that affect employee engagement and motivation, the most critical factor is that they are progressing in meaningful work. This research named this the progress principle. This work further points out that, besides making progress, people want to feel valued. Employees believe that the compensation rewards directly measure how the organization values them.

Leaders must never forget that *human* assets are the only *company* assets that appreciate over time, so it's essential to treat them well.

Takeaways: Treat Employees as You Would Want Them to Treat Customers

Value Your Employees:

- Employees provide a major competitive advantage.
- They differentiate the company from the competition.
- Keep morale and motivation high.
- Respect all members of the team and ask for their input.
- All jobs are essential; ensure each knows the impact of their job.
- Ensure they are making progress on meaningful work.
- Ensure all are compensated fairly.

Remember:

- When people know you care, they go the extra mile.
- Just like customers, you want your employees to be delighted with your company.
- Human assets are the only assets that appreciate over time. So, treat them well.

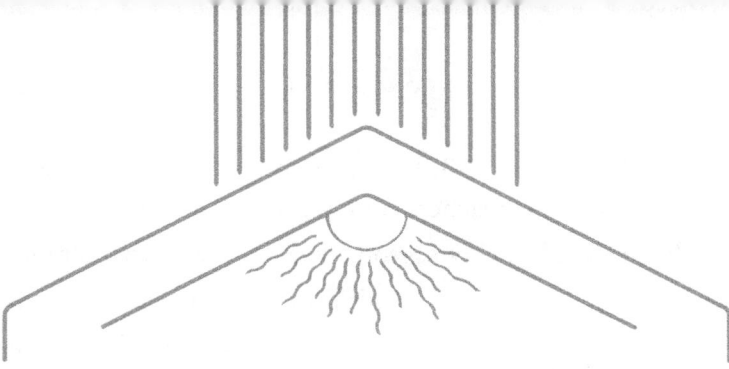

TOUCHSTONE #15

The More You Expect of People, the More They Achieve

Motivate people by expecting more of them.

People are genuinely encouraged by leaders who believe in them. It drives them to step up a level. Haven't you achieved more when you were expected to perform better? Speakers often perform better when in front of an audience than when practicing. This also holds for musicians and actors who perform better in front of an audience versus private rehearsals.

The so-called Pygmalion effect can explain this observation. In George Bernard Shaw's *Pygmalion*, Eliza Doolittle says that "the difference between a lady and a flower girl is not how she behaves but how she is treated." Classroom experiments in the 1960s (Rosenthal and Jacobson, 1968) demonstrated that the expectations of teachers toward students they considered promising affected students' performance. Two groups of students with similar average IQ scores were selected. The teachers were not informed of the scores but were told that one group had superior expectations compared with the other group. In the group for which the teacher had high expectations, the students performed significantly better than the other group of students for which the teacher had lower expectations.

Workplace studies (Livingston, 2003) showed that similar self-fulfilling prophecies also exist in businesses. These studies show that their expectations significantly influence how leaders treat their team members. Livingston cites several workplace examples demonstrating this effect. The research shows that the impact is related less to what the leaders and managers say but more to their subtle and often unintentional behavior.

> People are genuinely encouraged by leaders who believe in them.

Often, leaders need to communicate their positive feelings more clearly. Ensuring their best performers understand how they feel about their work is vital. This needs to be done continuously rather than once a year at the formal performance appraisal. Additional studies (Brafman and Brafman, 2008) show other examples of how positive and negative labels placed on people have short-term and long-term effects on their performance, behavior, and health. These studies illustrate that we can take on the characteristics others ascribe to us.

Of course, the expectations communicated to the team must be viewed as realistic and achievable. Even if they are possible, the workforce must believe they are viable. So, when setting the expectations, effective communication is essential. Miscommunication here can lead to high attrition rates or at least inhibit motivation. Research has shown (Atkinson, 1964) that the workforce becomes unmotivated when an expectation is perceived as either inevitable or impossible.

Takeaways: The More You Expect of People, the More They Achieve

- Remember the Pygmalion effect: High expectations of someone can be a self-fulfilling prophecy.
- Leaders can drive performance by convincing the team that they can perform to greater heights.
- Create a climate of respect and trust in which all can excel.
- Give team members more opportunities to contribute.
- Offer more detailed and more personalized feedback.
- Make your expectations realistic and achievable.
- Sending signals of low expectations can lower performance.

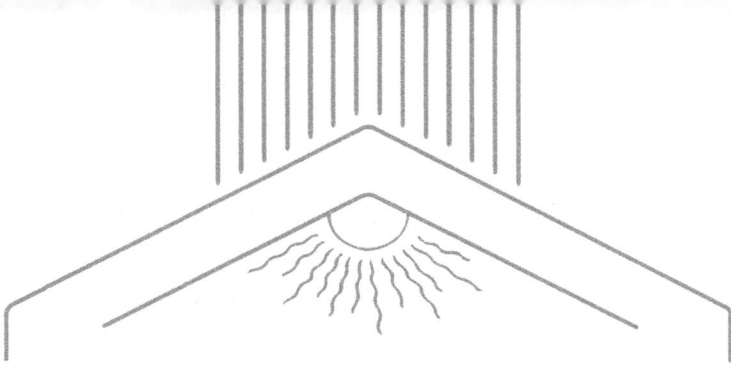

TOUCHSTONE #16

"No Deal" Is Better Than a "Bad Deal"

Agreements work best when all parties involved feel they achieved a fair deal, and all parties are satisfied with what they have received in the contract.

Achieving a "win-win" agreement requires "no deal" to be an option. Pursuing win-win agreements is not a technique but a philosophy. It requires an abundance mentality. All parties to the agreement must believe there is enough to satisfy all parties. The "pie" is not fixed but can grow if the deal is right. Zero-sum thinking, or a scarcity mentality, will always drive to a win-lose mentality (Covey, 1992).

Part of entering negotiations with "no deal" as an option is to have a Plan B if you find it necessary to walk away. Good leaders always think in terms of alternatives in the event of a failure. They must be able to pivot in a different direction immediately when they see their primary path being blocked.

Understanding that a win-win deal is not a compromise of principles or values is important. All parties must be satisfied and comfortable with the agreement, or it will break down in some fashion. Deals will have long-term effects one way or another. Even if the immediate deal is a short-term agreement, its success or failure will affect the following deal with the same or different parties. Word spreads, and others will be wary of your motivations if you compromise your integrity to achieve a win-lose situation. A good guideline is that if one party feels they have lost something, they should opt for "no deal."

> Agreements work best when all parties involved feel they achieved a fair deal, and all parties are satisfied with what they have received in the contract.

During the agreement discussions and negotiations, several warning signs may indicate you should consider "no deal" as an option. This includes the following factors:

- The other party or parties appear to need help living up to the proposed terms.

- Other opportunities to achieve the same goals are better than the proposed terms.

- Being driven to terms inconsistent with your minimum expectations.

- Potential long-term issues increase the risk of the agreement beyond your comfort zone or your ability to mitigate the risk adequately.

Finally, not getting *everything* one wants is not a loss. Sometimes, what we want is unattainable under the current circumstances. So, we must find a way to live with these realistic situations or be willing to walk away.

Takeaways: "No Deal" Is Better Than a "Bad Deal"

Win-Win Deals Aren't Compromises:

- Negotiating a "win-win" agreement requires "no deal" as an option.

- Win-win is not a technique but a philosophy.

- Win-win deals require an abundance mentality.

- All parties must be comfortable with the deal, or it will never work.

- If one of the parties (or more) feels they have lost something, they should opt for no deal.

We Don't Always Get What We Want:

- This doesn't amount to a loss.

- It is never necessary to compromise our principles.

- Sometimes, what we want is unattainable under the current circumstances.

- We must learn to walk away.

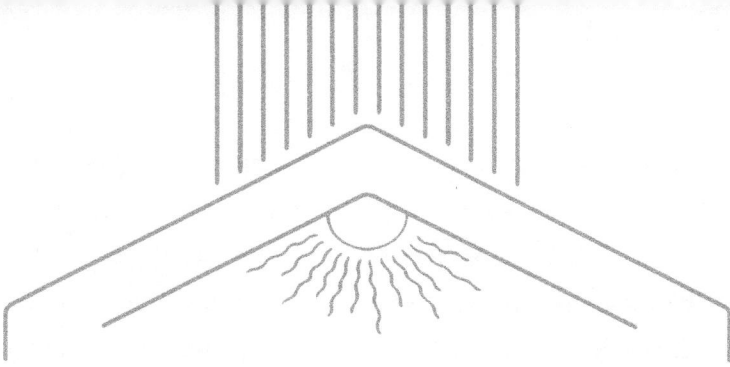

TOUCHSTONE #17

Fear of Loss Often Results in Irrational Decisions

Have you ever wondered why skilled and experienced people can make irrational decisions or exhibit irrational behavior? Why do some reject an excellent, economically sound offer that will profit them? Does it trouble you that managers often have pronounced blind spots?

In their book, *Sway: The Irresistible Pull of Irrational Behavior*, the Brafman brothers explore these questions (Brafman and Brafman, 2008). Irrational behavior among otherwise rational, intelligent, and well-trained people is driven by situations or conditions that block the normal, logical thought process. These situations sway people to react in specific ways because they trigger psychological undercurrents, often deep below the surface of our everyday activities. We can summarize these as follows:

- *Fear of loss*: It is often difficult to accept an impending loss. For example, we tend to hold on to an investment when the risk is inevitable and continues to grow and grow. When it is crystal clear that we should liquidate the sinking asset and salvage some value, we often hold on to it, wishing it will recover magically. Surprisingly, we become more loss averse when the potential loss is more significant. In business situations, the near-term aspect of the loss triggers irrational behavior. The best way to avoid the fear of loss is to have a long-term plan. This will provide the vision to avoid doing something foolish to avoid a near-term loss.

- *Commitment*: Recognizing a better alternative when fervently committed to a particular decision or position is difficult. This commitment will block the will to change, even when a better idea or position is evident to a neutral observer. Often the commitment is related to previous success. A successful marketing approach for your product starts to deteriorate because customers no longer relate to the message. But those who invented this approach attribute the sales reduction to anything but the marketing approach. This commitment to past success creates a blind spot for the leader, who resists change. It turns out that when fear of loss and commitment are coupled, the force that promotes irrational behavior increases its strength dramatically.

- *Value attribution*: The forces of influence or sway are also prevalent based on how something is labeled, by whom it is labeled or endorsed, or how much it may cost. Rather than objective data, perceived value often sways us to give someone or something certain qualities. Even the scientific community will give more credence to a finding by a renowned scholar than to someone new to the field without those credentials. The Brafman brothers give several examples of this behavior. Also, they demonstrate that when people receive a discount on a product or service, they value it less than if they paid full price. Value attribution is often coupled with commitment, resulting in further increased pull to irrational behavior.

- *Diagnosis bias*: Another psychological reaction related to value attribution is the strong tendency of people to evaluate others or ideas based on their initial opinions of them. These initial value judgments seem to be embedded so much that it is tough to reconsider them. This condition is often referred to as diagnosis bias. The Brafman brothers give several examples demonstrating that diagnosis bias is extreme in driving irrational decisions. One striking example is the strong correlation of the NBA draft pick number with playing time, as opposed to actual performance on the basketball court. Once the draft is over, the pick number should be inconsequential, but statistically, it isn't. Diagnosis bias is the basis behind the famous, albeit redundant, expression: "You only get one chance to make a good first impression."

- *Chameleon effect*: Value attribution and diagnosis bias affect each other, albeit subtly, in our everyday interactions. This leads to us taking on the characteristics that others attribute to us. Studies (Brafman and Brafman, 2008) have shown that negative feelings about aging can contribute to memory loss and even physical aging. So, we can all become chameleons in a psychological sense.

- *Fairness*: People's decisions are often connected to whether they are treated fairly. Even if it may benefit them financially, some may not accept an offer if they feel they were not treated fairly, making the decision appear irrational. That is why the nature of the process is so very often important when transacting business.

- *Altruism versus self-interest*: Why does a small token amount of money often demotivate people to help someone versus being asked to do the task as a favor? This seems irrational as one would think that a small sum would be preferred to nothing. It turns out that the altruism center and the self-interest (often called "pleasure") center of the brain cannot work simultaneously. If there is no monetary reward, the altruism center is deeply engaged, and the person's satisfaction comes from being altruistic. A minimal monetary reward triggers the pleasure center, which dismisses it because of the small amount. Since both centers cannot work simultaneously, altruistic satisfaction does not occur, and the task demotivates the person. Similarly, the pleasure center will always win when large bonuses are offered to meet performance targets. Therefore, the performance metrics must be appropriately defined. Otherwise, these incentives can lead to unintended consequences.

- *Dissent*: The psychological forces discussed previously can distort people's thinking in many ways when working in groups or teams, so much so that sometimes their behavior can become somewhat irrational. There must be trust among the teammates and a process that allows, even encourages, dissent. Without accepting and considering dissent, the team will follow the lead of the strongest personality of the group. Team members will assume one of the four roles: *initiator, blocker, supporter,* or *observer*. When the initiator pushes a new idea or direction, a blocker (dissenter) must challenge the concept and ensure that debate happens, and the correct path is chosen. If the team ignores or does not tolerate dissent, disastrous results can occur.

It is important to remember that people will always be influenced by psychological forces that can create irrational behavior. So, we need to recognize that by understanding these psychological influences, we can work to offset their power.

Takeaways: Fear of Loss Often Results in Irrational Decisions

Potential Losses Can Cause Overreaction:

- People tend to focus only on short-term consequences.
- The greater the potential loss, the more loss averse.
- Perceived value replaces objective data.
- Loss aversion + commitment yields irrationality.
- A long-term plan helps avoid the irrational pull.

Other Important Factors:

- Strong commitment creates blind spots.
- Initial opinions create labels on people and things.
- Value attribution and diagnosis bias can drive irrationality.
- Metrics for monetary incentives must be carefully chosen.
- Dissent is invaluable for inhibiting irrational behavior.
- Dissenters expand discussion, allowing various viewpoints.

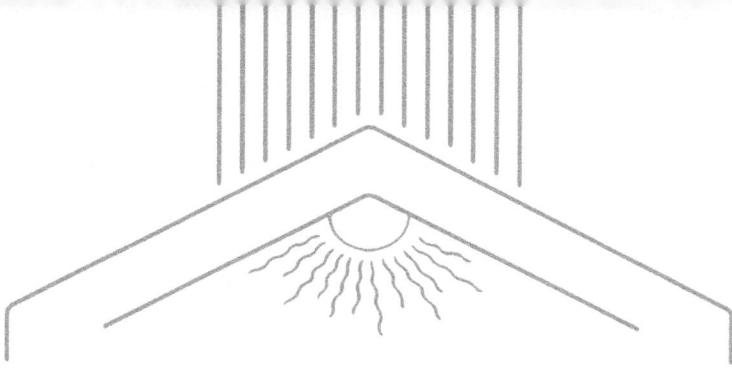

TOUCHSTONE #18

Trust Is the Highest Form of Human Motivation

One of the hallmarks of a good leader is a high level of trust demonstrated within the leader's organization at all levels, both internally and with external stakeholders. Stephen Covey's son (Covey, 2006) dedicates an entire book to the subject of trust.

Why is trust so important? When trust is high, everything in business moves much faster. When people feel trusted, they are highly motivated. One of the best motivators is to trust people with meaningful projects that play to their talents. Trust also brings out the best in people. It overcomes the human tendency to avoid difficult topics. This produces a significant differentiator in the business world. High-trust organizations require much less bureaucracy. Decisions can be made much faster; more importantly, these decisions are more readily accepted and supported by the workforce. This continues to build a strong team-based culture.

Individual trustworthiness requires both character and competence. Many people give their complete trust to someone because of their impeccable character. While character is essential, we can only fully trust someone who is also competent. That is why it is so important to have all our good people placed in the proper role that plays to their strengths and inborn talents, not their weaknesses.

> One of the hallmarks of a good leader is a high level of trust demonstrated within the leader's organization at all levels, both internally and with external stakeholders.

High trust throughout an organization will create communication channels that are efficient, effective, and quick. Even poorly phrased communications will be interpreted correctly. On the contrary, in low-trust environments, even very carefully constructed communications will be misinterpreted negatively. As the business cycle moves faster and faster, trust in an organization leads to a significant competitive advantage. Bureaucracy is reduced. Let's face it: bureaucracy grows when there is no trust. Many policies were put there because trust was violated, by character flaws, competence failures, or both. Well-deserved trust, on the contrary, creates efficiencies that

- improve quality.

- remove wasted time and energy.

- increase customer satisfaction.

- lower cost.

Therefore, trust creates a dividend for the company, improving stakeholder returns. A primary job of leaders is to inspire trust throughout their organizations. To do this requires the leader not only to be trustworthy (possess character and competence) but also to be credible. Gaining credibility requires demonstrating the following characteristics:

- integrity through honesty and adherence to principles

- motive based on mutual benefit

- capability that inspires confidence

- performance with a track record of results

Teaching and mentoring increase trust. These activities provide confidence in people as they understand you care. They eliminate the suspicion that can be formed by those who lack trust in the company. Often, it is better to trust colleagues until they prove themselves unworthy of that trust. If that happens, action must be taken. Furthermore, trust but verify often helps the relationship.

Takeaways: Trust Is the Highest Form of Human Motivation

Trust Is Everything:

- In high-trust organizations, everything moves faster and is more efficient.
- Trusting people with meaningful projects brings out the best in people.
- It's important to assign projects based on strengths and talents.
- The first job of a leader is to inspire trust.
  - This requires character and competence.
  - Lack of either destroys trust.

Trust Establishes Credibility:

- The credibility of the leadership is imperative to inspire trust.
- Integrity is about honesty and adherence to principles.
  - Motive is based on mutual benefit.
  - Capability inspires confidence.
  - Performance is measured by a track record of results.
- Companies high in trust gain a performance dividend, while low trust yields a performance loss.
- Trust until someone proves unworthy of that trust.
- Trusting, but verifying, often helps the relationship if done correctly.

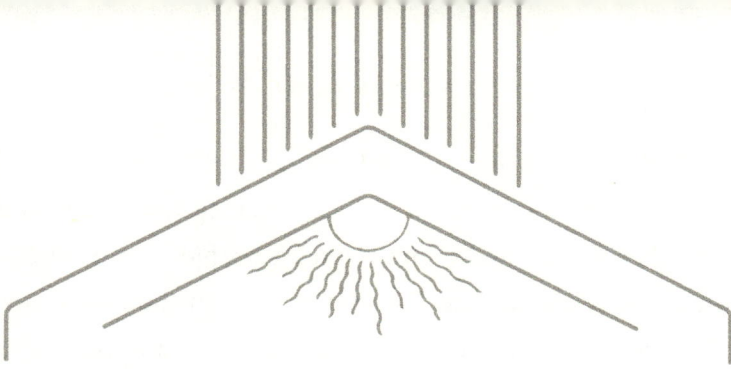

TOUCHSTONE #19

Keep Those Who Hate You Away from Those Who Haven't Made Up Their Minds

Hate is a *lack of trust.*

In an organization, there will be people who don't trust you as the leader. So, when introducing new players into the organization, it is essential not to let the "distrusters" significantly influence those who haven't had a chance to evaluate the leadership objectively. Psychological studies have shown that once people firmly make up their minds, it is difficult to get them to change. That is why creating an environment where new employees will keep an open mind is so important.

Of course, this initially sounds like a challenging task. But it is essential to be aware that, as a leader, you must provide a way to get distrusters to a level of understanding of the mission so that they are reluctant to undermine the agenda of change to improve the organization. This keeps all the relationships less personal and more focused on the merits of the business strategy. Remember, the objective is not to get them all to like you but to respect and trust you in leading the business and that you care about their livelihood.

In Jim Collins's *Good to Great* (Collins, 2001), "getting the right people on the bus" is presented as a key to exceptional performance. Knowing that there may be some "wrong people," those who don't support the strategy and the mission, already on the bus, you want to make sure that the right people aren't influenced improperly and become distrusters. So, consider these matters when structuring the reporting relationships and assigning roles and responsibilities. In the long run, we must find ways to get the wrong people off the bus.

It is often difficult to identify the haters in an organization. Some may be obvious, but many are hard to find because they lack transparency. These individuals typically have passive-aggressive tendencies. Once, I moved into a new position as president of a new subsidiary. The head of Human Resources was quite receptive on the surface but privately strongly resisted the changes we needed to make to move the company to the next level. In our meetings, this very competent individual agreed to our strategy and pledged support. But then, none of his commitments were accomplished.

Hate is a *lack of trust.*

Unfortunately, he always gave reasons for why things were not happening. These always pointed to impediments created by other departments or external requirements. There was no buy-in to the strategy. This is often the case with employees who do not trust the strategy or leadership. Once we recognized this passive-aggressive behavior, we discussed our concerns privately and listened to his ideas and concerns.

As a result, we were able to turn this situation around before others in the company assimilated any negativity from this individual. It turns out that the prior leader of the organization would not listen to the HR leader's ideas and concerns, creating this lack of trust. It was fortunate that the situation turned around, and it shows the importance of identifying the haters early and dealing with the situation. Looking for illogical performance issues, resistance to change, and passive-aggressive behavior is essential in determining the individuals causing underlying problems that hurt the company's overall performance.

In addition to driving home the strategy and mission to convert the detractors, trying to be more human can strongly affect them, and being somewhat less serious at times will be helpful. Also, it is important to improve communication by ensuring people aren't pitted against one another.

Most likely, you won't be able to convert or remove all the detractors, especially in larger organizations, so expect some sabotage, especially in unnecessary delays in implementing changes or passive-aggressive behavior. It is essential to recognize that rational thinking and debate will not work with people who don't embrace change.

Takeaways: Keep Those Who Hate You Away from Those Who Haven't Made Up Their Minds

- In this context, hate is defined as a lack of trust in the company's leadership.
- Help detractors to understand the mission.
- Being more human will win over *some* detractors.
  - Avoid being too serious.
  - Improve communication to ensure people aren't pitted against one another.
  - Good leaders are also good followers.
- Expect some sabotage, and remember you will never convert all detractors.
- Rational thinking will not work with people who won't embrace change.

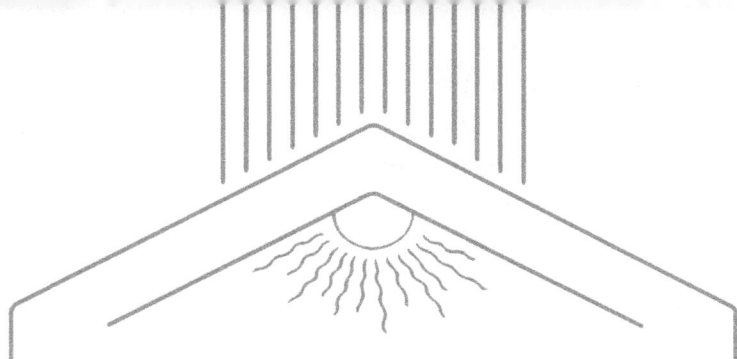

TOUCHSTONE #20

Hate Is Difficult the Closer You Get to Someone

When people feel displeasure with others or with policies, processes, or organizations, they often erect barriers to avoid displeasure, even though they may not understand the reasons for their unpleasant or uncomfortable feelings.

These barriers provide a protective shield, or at least people believe they do, making them more self-centered. In addition to these barriers inhibiting any real form of collaboration, they can result in hatred and resentment. The hate continues to get stronger and stronger as the distance between the parties increases, both in space and in time, so much so that communication is essentially reduced to zero.

Leaders need to recognize this early so that there is a chance to repair the situation before it becomes irreparable. It is also important to note that fear can also breed hate. These hate or lack-of-trust situations often arise in companies undergoing rapid changes. The change agents within the company driving the change are the targets of this lack of trust.

Of course, the CEO is one of the primary targets because they are the leader and supporter of the changes. The staff assigned to drive the change throughout the organization are also often targets. Chief information officers (CIOs) are frequently the target of hate because information technology (IT) is rapidly changing in many companies as they strive to compete.

As CIOs introduce new major systems, such as supply chains, inventory, and customer relations, sold to everyone as the panacea to solve all the problems, people are skeptical but initially get on board. When the systems don't meet expectations, much of the workforce blames the CIO, and the hate begins. People stop communicating with the CIO, and the blame game begins—the people who can help this situation get farther apart.

> A lack of trust between individuals or between a person and the organization typically drives the hate.

But the company's culture and capability often cause problems, not the IT tool chosen and implemented. For example, many customer relationship management systems do not meet expectations because the company has no customer relationship culture or strategy. There is often no plan. IT tools are only as good as the user. It is interesting to note that the average tenure of a CIO is roughly three years (Riazi, 2022).

The best solution to alleviate this lack of trust in a business environment is to draw the person or situation closer. A lack of trust between individuals or between a person and the organization typically drives the hate. Remedying these situations takes time and a lot of patience. It often requires unconditional friendliness on a very frequent basis.

As you work to bring the parties closer, try to empathize. It is essential to focus on the good things the parties have accomplished and highlight the expected new achievements. Things must always be kept at a highly professional level, and it is important to work on transforming enemies into friends. While you may never get there completely, the attempt will reduce the feelings of hatred from both directions.

Takeaways: Hate Is Difficult the Closer You Get to Someone

Break Down Barriers:

- People often erect barriers if they experience displeasure with persons, policies, or processes.
- The barriers can turn into hatred.
- The hatred strengthens as the distance, in space and time, increases.
- Fear can also breed hate.

Draw Closer:

- In a business situation, the solution is to draw closer.
- Focus on patience and unconditional friendliness.
- Overcome the fear of pain or displeasure.
- As you work at getting closer, try to empathize.
  - Look at the good things the person does.
  - Keep it on a professional level.
- Transform enemies into friends.

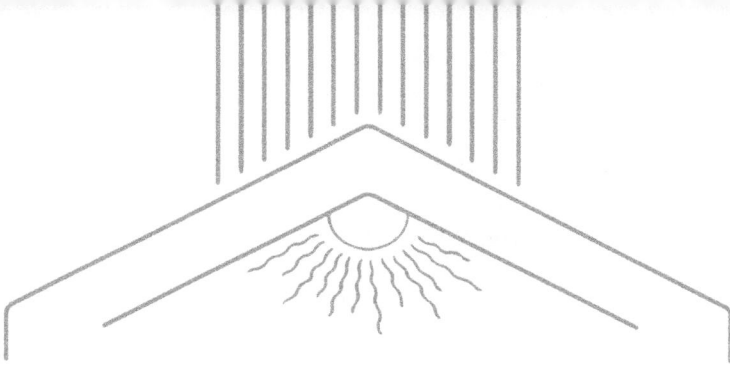

TOUCHSTONE #21

Leaders Strive to Be Respected, Not to Be Loved

Effective business leadership is about something other than giving speeches or being liked; leadership is defined by lasting results, not attributes (Drucker, 2006).

Of course, it is always nice if you can have both, but respect is essential and is driven by the organization achieving results that engender pride by all in the organization. Leaders will have to make tough decisions to achieve exceptional results, and some people won't agree and may be upset by these decisions. The leaders must explain the rationale for the decision, listen to feedback, and truly evaluate their ideas and complaints.

At all costs, however, the leader must not avoid making the decision. The leader must put the final decision in the context of benefit to the entire company and emphasize that the team must win as a team, not as individuals. It takes true self-confidence and emotional intelligence (Goleman, 1996) to make these tough decisions and hold the team together. Leaders who strongly desire to be liked will take shortcuts. They will avoid the sticky issues and even compromise principles.

To be respected, you should

- always deliver more than promised.

- respect yourself with confidence and understand no one is perfect.

- bring people together.

- fix the problems; don't fix the blame.

- create a learning organization.

- praise accomplishments publicly; criticize privately.

- learn to love change.

Also, while building the organization, it is essential to relate to the individuals, but a certain distance must be maintained to be respected. In the words of the famous football coach of the Green Bay Packers, Vince Lombardi, "The leader can never close the gap between himself and the group. If he does, he is no longer what he must be. He must walk a tightrope between the consent he must win and the control he must exert."

> Leadership is defined by lasting results, not attributes.

This is not to say that people skills and emotional intelligence are unimportant, especially as a leader moves up through the organization. Placing respect ahead of being liked does not mean one can ignore the talent and skill to relate to and motivate people. Respect (and stellar results) will only come if the leader has developed emotional competencies, such as regulating negative emotions during crises, negotiating with peers, and building support for change (Bunker et al., 2002).

Takeaways: Leaders Strive to Be Respected, Not to Be Loved

- Leadership is defined by results, not attributes.
  - Making tough decisions will upset some people.
  - The leader's job is to define the rationale for the decision.
  - Decisions must be put in the context of the entire group.
  - The team must win, not a department or function.
- True self-confidence and emotional intelligence are needed to hold the team together.
- When there is a strong desire to be liked, leaders may
  - take shortcuts.
  - avoid the "sticky issues" and even compromise principles.
- To be respected:
  - always deliver more than promised—don't leave anyone hanging.
  - respect yourself with confidence; no one is perfect.
  - bring people together with warmth.
  - fix the problems; don't fix the blame.
  - create a learning organization.
  - praise accomplishments publicly; criticize privately.
  - love change and lead the change process.
- The gap between the leader and the group must never be closed.

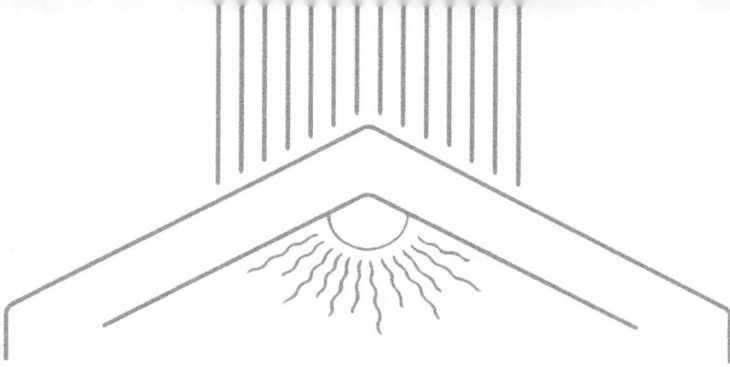

TOUCHSTONE #22

The Human Soul Hungers to Be Appreciated, Valued, and Recognized

Interpersonal relationships within an organization will become strong when we appreciate, value, and recognize our colleagues and associates (Covey, 1992).

If this is not happening in your organization, severe conflicts and a significant lack of trust will emerge. Recognizing achievement in an organization can become very difficult because the recognition must be sincere in the minds and hearts of the entire workforce. Recognition programs tend to fall short. For example, employee-of-the-month programs often become political or perceived as political and can breed a lack of trust.

In general, programs tend to work poorly when driving a cultural change in an organization. Programs tend to produce short-term progress, but the changes never last. That is because actual cultural change requires large majorities of the organization to internalize the changes. People must feel that the changes have improved things for all stakeholders (employees, customers, suppliers, owners, and the community). This takes significant amounts of time and consistent reinforcement of the ideas.

It takes work to develop a culture where people genuinely want to see one another be successful. It requires the entire leadership team to listen intently and with genuine empathy. Empathy is the ability to sense another's feelings and seriously consider those feelings, among other factors, when making decisions. This will have a significant effect if the other person senses that you truly feel what they are feeling and that you care. It is essential to listen, ask intelligent questions, and project warmth until the other person thinks they are understood. This is a critical dimension of the concept of emotional intelligence (Goleman, 1996).

> Interpersonal relationships within an organization will become strong when we appreciate, value, and recognize our colleagues and associates.

In addition to listening, expressing appreciation is a way to develop a culture of respect. Introducing a practice of personal notes is especially effective (Porath and Pearson, 2013). These notes are handy when you appreciate someone as a role model, praising their work ethic or pointing out their ability to excel under the most challenging conditions. In this digital age, a personal handwritten note of appreciation accentuates the effect of the message. I have heard people say, "She actually took the time to handwrite this; she must really mean it."

When you visit a company for the first time and see cheerful and smiling workers, it almost always positively affects you. Companies have a culture in which their people are appreciated, valued, and recognized by the leadership and one another. So, as you facilitate positive culture change, leaders should smile often.

This behavior will become contagious, and over time, it will help improve the culture significantly.

Takeaways: The Human Soul Hungers to Be Appreciated, Valued, and Recognized

- Develop a culture that supports positive reinforcement of people's achievements.
  - Attitudes must recognize appreciation for one another.
  - Strong desire to help one another to be successful.
- Become a good listener.
  - Listen until the other person feels understood.
  - Empathize when you listen; this makes people feel appreciated.
  - Ask questions and summarize what they said.
- Recognition programs tend to be short-term fixes and often are considered political and unfair.
- Personal notes of appreciation are often very effective.
- Smiling appropriately sends a feeling of warmth and trust.

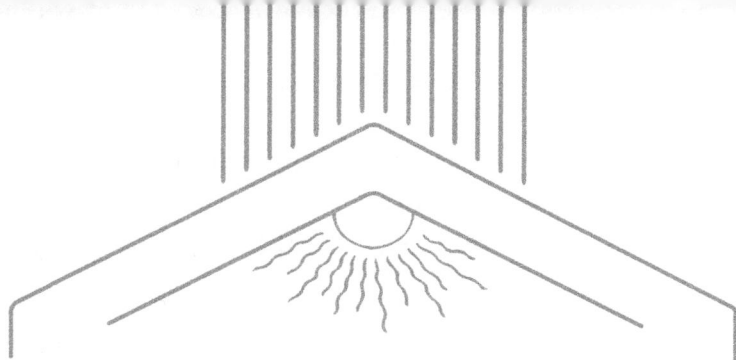

TOUCHSTONE #23

A Formula for Failure Is to Try to Please Everybody All the Time

Herbert Bayard Swope, Sr., a Pulitzer Prize–winning reporter for the *New York World*, first stated this Touchstone. He affirmed that when we try to please everyone all the time, we wind up pleasing no one, including ourselves.

No one will truly know where the leader stands on certain issues. The last one in the room with this type of leader will often get their way. This behavior will most assuredly lead to decreased morale, demotivation, and failures in the business.

Leadership requires making difficult decisions that are often unpleasant for coworkers but necessary for the business to be successful. The key is encouraging ideas, objections, and alternatives to the surface, being heard, and being thoroughly evaluated. People must truly feel that their opinions were honestly considered. Then, make the final decision and logically explain the rationale and reasons. The leader must be firm and convincing. It is essential to call for unity to support the decision.

Remember, if the easy decisions get to the top of the organization to solve, someone is dropping the ball. The leader must refrain from making suboptimum decisions on an important matter to appease the objections of a few with only the intention of pleasing them. If the leader bends or waffles, all will see the need for more commitment. No one will be happy, and the business will lose its direction.

> Leadership requires making difficult decisions that are often unpleasant for coworkers but necessary for the business to be successful.

Creative or visionary ideas are often unpopular when first introduced. People are often frightened by innovative ideas, and this leads to resistance. Some become unhappy and resist further when these ideas move into concrete plans and projects. The leader who believes these new ideas will improve the company must press forward with their convictions despite the criticisms from those who object. The leader must bring those objectors along or find a way to separate them from the organization.

Takeaways: A Formula for Failure Is to Try to Please Everybody All the Time

- Trying to please everyone leads to pleasing no one, including ourselves.
  - It leads to lower morale, demotivation, and failure.
  - No one knows where the leader truly stands on certain issues.
- Creative and visionary ideas are often met with resistance.
  - The leader must stand firm in the face of criticism.
- The key is to listen to all voices and opinions on important matters.
  - Make a final decision and call for unity.
  - Don't suboptimize to make the critics happy.

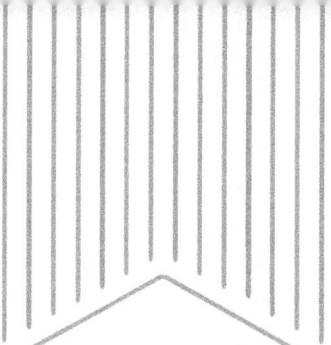

PART 3
Managerial Skills

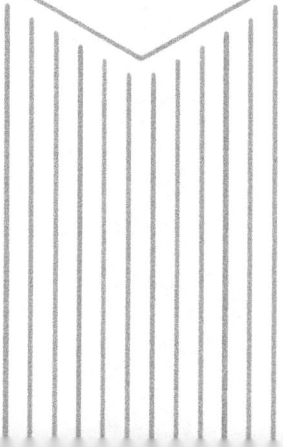

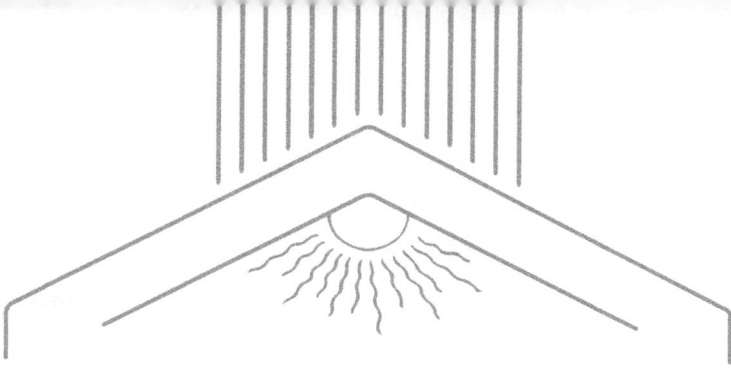

TOUCHSTONE # 24

A-Players Hire A-Players; B-Players Hire C-Players

While this Touchstone has been attributed to many business leaders, it is most often attributed to Donald Rumsfeld, as it is one of Rumsfeld's Rules (Rumsfeld, 2013). "Surround yourself with top-notch people; success depends on it" is the guidance most often given to executives taking over a new organization, starting a new business venture, or developing a new product. This also provides an excellent path for developing a successor.

A-players tend to seek excellence, which attracts other A-players. This drives the business toward an authentic culture of excellence, whereas B-players hire C-players. Looking at the team surrounding a leader will be a strong indicator of which leaders are A-players and who are B-players. B-players are often insecure, making hiring people who might outperform them uncomfortable. In reality, leaders are highly recognized for picking the best people.

Screening for talent, character, and fit is essential in finding A-players. Talent should not be confused with knowledge or skills. Talent is a recurring thought, feeling, or behavior that can be productively applied (Buckingham and Coffman, 1999). Talent, as defined here, cannot be taught or learned; it can only be improved. The basic tendencies must be there from the beginning and in the DNA program, so to speak. A strong desire for precision is a talent. That desire cannot be learned. To be an excellent accountant, one must have this talent of loving precision. The need to be of service, the need to be on stage, the need to be seen as competent, and the need to help others grow are all examples of talents. Buckingham and Coffman give a detailed explanation of talent and examples of how these talents create a productive environment in many different circumstances. The bottom line is that excellence is only possible with talent. And everyone has talent in some way, shape, or form.

> Talent should not be confused with knowledge or skills.

Based on this, it becomes evident that the leader must find the proper match between the talent and the employee's role if they are to be an A-player. Fit, however, has a second requirement for building the right organization. There is also a fit to match the organization's culture, especially with the future culture that the leader is nurturing. Two aspects of fit, the fit of role and culture, are necessary ingredients to develop an excellent team.

Top-notch A-players must also have character. Leaders need to be able to trust their supporting team implicitly. The leader cannot be following up on every little item. Honesty and integrity throughout the team will enable the leader to trust everyone and rest assured that they will act in the best interests of all the company's stakeholders legally and forthrightly.

Takeaways: A-Players Hire A-Players; B-Players Hire C-Players

A-Players:

- Surround themselves with top-notch talent.
- Realize that success depends upon their team.

B-Players:

- Tend to be insecure.
- Are not comfortable hiring people who may outperform them.

Keys to Finding A-Players:

- Hire for talent, character, and fit.
  - Talent: Look for a recurring pattern of thought, feeling, or behavior that can be productively applied.
  - Character: Watch for integrity and honesty.
  - Fit: See if they are a good fit with the role and with the culture.
- Most people want to do what they are good at doing.

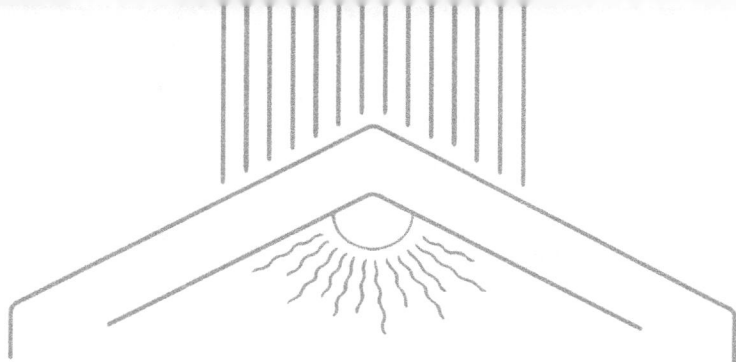

TOUCHSTONE #25

Never Negotiate against Yourself

Many tend to think of a contract negotiation where the terms and price are hammered out between the parties over the delivery of goods and services. But this is a very narrow viewpoint. In reality, we negotiate with everyone we meet throughout the business day, such as colleagues, customers, and suppliers.

The key point of this Touchstone is to never negotiate against yourself during any of these interactions. This internal debate that happens before you interact on very important topics is essential to get things started on a winning path (Fox, 2013). You must always be aware that negotiation is an emotional process that can be subject to irrationality.

The most vivid examples of potentially negotiating against yourself are explained in the world of contract negotiation. In one's personal life, negotiation against yourself can happen without realizing it. For example, many folks are reluctant to "put it on the line." They fear making statements like, "I'll buy that car right now if you discount it by 33 percent." Instead, they negotiate against themselves by convincing themselves that the car dealer will never accept such an offer.

Negotiating against yourself is not relegated to a purchase transaction. Suppose a unique position opens in another department. Some people won't apply because they think it is wired for someone else. Or they think the manager prefers to go outside to bring in some new blood. Or they will construct another reason so that they don't have to put themselves through the evaluation process. In essence, they are negotiating with themselves.

The process is usually subtler in business-to-business negotiations, but "self-negotiation" can often happen. For example, a customer, in response to your proposal, says, "You are our preferred supplier, but to award this contract to your company, I need you to sharpen your pencil a bit." You then respond with a good gesture and lower your bid. Then, some time goes by, and you finally hear back. Now there is some new issue which triggers a new requirement to lower your price again. So, you respond with a

> The best negotiators are excellent listeners.

slightly lower bid. You just negotiated against yourself twice! This is not a good-faith negotiation. You deserve a firm counteroffer to your original bid. No one should be expected to provide a new bid without a firm counteroffer. It is essential to stop this behavior, not only for purchase contract negotiations but also for all types of negotiations.

It turns out that the best negotiators are excellent listeners. To reach an agreement where both parties feel comfortable and satisfied, empathetic listening will find ways to provide value to the other party without compromising what is essential to you. This works especially well for more complex negotiations where some terms and conditions are very important in addition to price. For example, delivery schedule flexibility on the buyer's part can often allow the seller to produce more efficiently and thus may enable the seller to meet the buyer's target price. Custom packaging can be another area that can work for both parties. These kinds of "requirements behind the requirements" can be identified by listening and asking great questions during the process.

In essence, life is a negotiation (Voss, 2016). In both our personal and work lives, many of our day-to-day interactions are negotiations. That is why it is so important that we understand how to interact both in gathering information (listening) and in influencing behavior.

Takeaways: Never Negotiate against Yourself

- We negotiate with many people each day on many different things.
- People often convince themselves that the other party won't accept their offer.
- In B2B, negotiating against yourself is a bit more subtle.
  - You'll be told to keep sharpening your pencil.
  - Before giving another offer, the other party should make a good-faith offer for you to consider.
  - Don't work with someone who continually wants reductions.
- Never counter your own offer.
- The best negotiators are good listeners.
- Provide value to the other party without compromising what is essential to you.

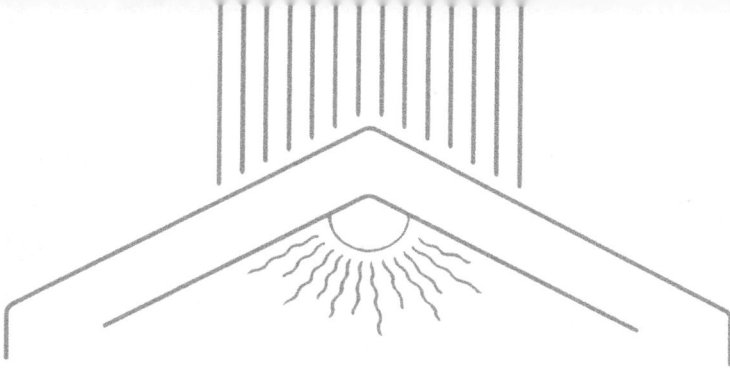

TOUCHSTONE #26

Never Negotiate "Line-by-Line" and "Bottom-Line" Simultaneously

Cost and price negotiations often take one of two paths: line-by-line or bottom-line.

In the line-by-line approach, the negotiators review the major contractual tasks; discuss the scope of each task, the people assigned, and the purchased materials required; and debate the cost or price of each line item or task. The idea is that once the negotiators haggle out their differences on each line item, it becomes a simple addition to get to the total or bottom-line price for the contract.

In the bottom-line approach, the negotiators focus on the overall goals, objectives, and deliverables under the scope of the contract and directly address the total price. They often use similar contracts as benchmarks and adjust the price accordingly. They also often use competitive pricing as a starting point.

Problems occur when you start with the line-by-line approach but the total price by adding each line item does not match the buyer's expectations. The buyer then switches to the bottom-line approach, ignoring all the line-by-line work done. If this happens, the major problem from the seller's perspective is that the seller has already given up concessions on price and scope detail during the line-by-line discussions. Now, the buyer wants further concessions.

> Once you start line-by-line negotiations, the ground rule must be that both parties will live with the results.

At this point, the seller should not make bottom-line concessions. It is not fair for the buyer to expect that. This is unfair to the seller and wastes a lot of time for both parties. The only fair thing to do at this point is to go back to the line-by-line approach and see if the buyer can live with scope and schedule changes to allow the bottom-line price to come down to the expected amount.

Once you start line-by-line negotiations, the ground rule must be that both parties will live with the results. Unfortunately, few buyers will agree to this up front. One way to deal with this is for both parties to accept some risk on the outcome or a variable fee on the contract. This line-by-line versus bottom-line discussion also applies to schedule negotiations.

Takeaways: Never Negotiate "Line-by-Line" and "Bottom-Line" Simultaneously

Line-by-Line Approach:

- Discuss each major line-item task in the scope.

- Negotiate the price of each line item.

- Once settled, the total or bottom-line price is the sum of the negotiated price of each line item.

Bottom-Line Approach:

- Examine the contract scope in the aggregate or total scope.

- Use similar deals as benchmarks or competitive prices for comparison.

A Problem Occurs If:

- The line-by-line approach gives a bottom-line price inconsistent with expectations.

- The buyer tries to switch to the bottom-line approach. This is unfair to the seller because concessions have been made on each line. It also wastes a lot of time for both parties.

Live with the Results:

- Once line-by-line is chosen, both parties must agree to live with the results.

- Most buyers will not agree to this.

- Both parties must agree to accept some risk or liability on the outcome.

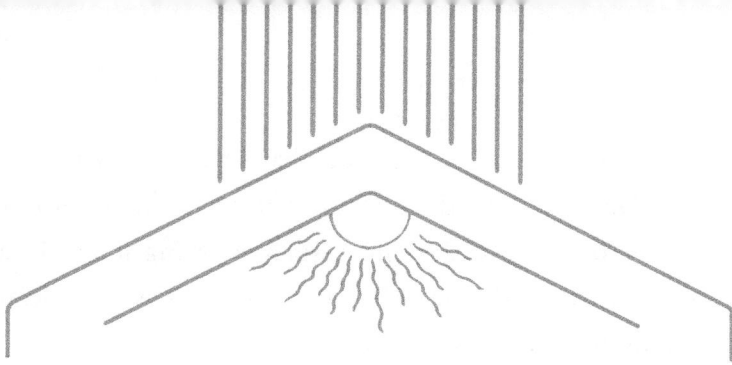

TOUCHSTONE # 27

Once You Get into a Hole, Stop Digging

This Touchstone has been attributed to several sources, including Will Rogers. The first written version of it appeared in the *Washington Post* in 1911. Other sources include Denis Healey, the British politician, and Donald Rumsfeld as one of Rumsfeld's Rules (Rumsfeld, 2013). It is often referred to as the *First Law of Holes*.

The fundamental definition of being in a hole is making the same mistake repeatedly. Sometimes, we don't even recognize we are in a hole. This is because we have blind spots. We think we are doing everything right and keep doing the same thing as things worsen. This could be due to a bad habit, a poor policy, poor implementation of a good strategy, or just a very poor strategy. In this sense, to continue digging means repeating the same activity and wishing the situation or result will improve.

Musicians understand this phenomenon very well. When learning a musical instrument, it is tempting to pass over a small mistake with the assumption you will correct it the next time you practice this piece. However, the same mistake occurs the second time, the third time, and the fourth time. Now, the mistake has been rehearsed, so it has become a habit. Now, it is much harder to get it correct. The proper approach is to take the difficult passage in the musical piece and attack it from a different angle, such as trying it slowly until it becomes mastered. The worst thing you can do as a musician or businessperson is practice mistakes.

In business situations, at some point, leaders must be objective and realize they are in a hole. Once you realize you are there, it may be hard to stop doing what got you into the hole. As in the musician analogy, you don't realize what is causing the problem. For example, when a product line is no longer selling, and you keep trying the same sales tactics, you are in a hole. Recognize it. Believe it. Stop using the same sales tactics. Another business example is increasing R&D spending and getting nowhere but continuing down the same path. Again, stopping spending, taking stock, and determining whether the entire strategy must be changed are important. Sometimes, the business is just working on the wrong things.

> The fundamental definition of being in a hole is making the same mistake repeatedly.

Of course, once you stop digging, you are still in a hole (some have called this the *Second Law of Holes*). The question is, *how do you climb out of the hole?* Root cause analysis provides a very reliable first step. Find out the cause or causes, and then develop a plan to eliminate them. In the case of the sales tactics example mentioned earlier, the following questions must be asked: *What can I do to differentiate my product from the competition? Is it contractual? Is it lead-time or schedule related? What is the competition doing better?* Sometimes, finding a way to leapfrog the issues is the best way out of the hole, which often entails changing strategy.

Takeaways: Once You Get into a Hole, Stop Digging

- Sometimes, we don't realize we are in a hole.
  - It may be hard to stop doing what got us into the hole.
  - Is it due to a bad habit or policy of the organization?
- We must be objective and realize that we are there.
- Once you stop digging, you are still in a hole.
  - Find the cause.
  - Develop an action plan to eliminate the cause or causes.
  - Another strategy is to leapfrog the issue.

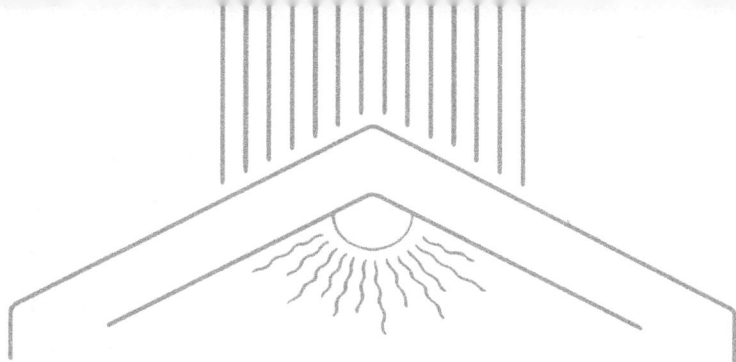

TOUCHSTONE #28

Don't Counter an Offer If You Can't Split the Difference

Some people say, "Never split the difference." It's even the title of a book on negotiation (Voss, 2016). But this Touchstone is directed at making a counteroffer and what that counteroffer should be. It does not imply you must split the difference. This Touchstone also implicitly acknowledges that a negotiation is a very emotional experience, and sound logic may not always be present.

Regardless of whether you pursue the rational problem-solving approach described in the book *Getting to Yes* (Fisher and Ury, 2011) or whether you use the more empathetic approach to negotiation described in *Never Split the Difference* (Voss, 2016) or a hybrid strategy developed within your company, the overarching goal will be the same—that is, an agreement that will be satisfactory and beneficial to both parties.

We should always strive for what has become known as a "win-win" agreement. This requires a focus on principles and not positions. This is tricky because negotiating in good faith and maintaining a relationship between the parties require some give-and-take. If you back yourself into a corner where you cannot adjust your terms, including price, it may kill the deal when there is a clear path to a good deal for both the parties.

> We should always strive for what has become known as a "win-win" agreement.

As the nonfinancial major terms and legal structure proceed, price structure often becomes a sticking point. Some negotiators try to finalize this up front, but in major deals, the nonfinancial aspects of the deal, such as schedule and overall scope, affect the price. Therefore, price structure is always a normalizing tool to settle other deal requirements.

We have seen deals fall apart at the very end because one of the parties cannot make a final price adjustment to close the deal. The emphasis or advice here is to ensure the negotiators are positioned so that there is enough flexibility to close the deal and not get backed into a corner during the negotiation process.

Takeaways: Don't Counter an Offer If You Can't Split the Difference

- Regardless of the negotiation approach, price is important.
- Some say, "Never split the difference." However, give-and-take will be required.
  - Splitting is one of the guiding principles in negotiation strategy.
  - Focus on principles and not positions.
  - "Splitting" should allow you to maintain a good relationship.
- Never counter with your final position.
- Always leave room for another round.
  - The amount of room should be midway between their offer and your counter.
- At any point in the negotiation, if the other side says, "Let's split the difference," you want to be able to say, albeit reluctantly, "Okay."
- Remember: The goal is to get to an agreement that meets your requirements and satisfies the interest of both parties.

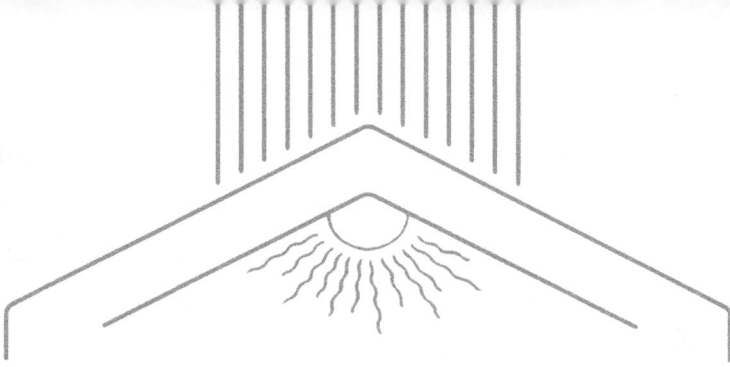

TOUCHSTONE #29

Problems Are Opportunities Dressed in Work Clothes

Life is opportunistic, as is business. Problems will occur in life and business. When these problems occur, our mindset determines whether we view them as opportunities or not. If we are pragmatic, we see that solving this problem will add value and is an opportunity.

Many do not attempt to solve problems directly because they fear failure. They think that their reputation will be harmed. It is just the opposite. *Not* trying creates a negative reputation. The person who doesn't try will be branded as someone who avoids difficult tasks and is unreliable. In contrast, the one who enters the arena will get the credit. It is important to show up and try (Roosevelt, 1910).

Another reason people often ignore problems is because solving them is hard work (Robinson, 2013). Hard work is the work that usually involves change, and change is hard. It requires us to change the way we think and change how we act. Turning problems into opportunities requires overcoming fear, making difficult decisions, and rising to the challenge.

Sometimes, we will falter, but success will start again after every failure. As Winston Churchill said, "Success is not final; failure is not fatal—it's the courage to continue that counts." The hard work of solving problems often involves working outside of your comfort zone. Mario Andretti, the famous race car driver, said, "If you feel like you are in control, you aren't going fast enough." Creating opportunities from difficulty often feels like that as well.

> Many do not attempt to solve problems directly because they fear failure.

Customer contractual problems are always tricky to solve. I recall a situation where a manufacturing company was very aggressive in a bid to manufacture a pharmaceutical ingredient that the customer was producing in-house. The customer decided to outsource this ingredient that went into their final product. This was a product that had been manufactured for many years.

After the transfer of the process to the manufacturing company, the company experienced financial losses on the ingredients. Their bid was too aggressive, and they were under contract for several more years to manufacture the product. Also, because of changes in ownership, a new president was appointed to run the manufacturing company. New management had to address this problem immediately—their goal being to solve the contractual issue without damaging their customer relationship, as they would depend on this customer for additional business on new products in the future.

The new president and his team developed a plan to solve the immediate problem of a loss contract and create a significant strategic opportunity for the future. The new president decided to meet with the customer's procurement head. He presented the details of the losses on the contract and demonstrated that it was not because of poor operations, but that the cost basis was impractical. The customer agreed to raise the price if the company were amenable to open-book pricing. The president agreed to this unprecedented request. The contract was amended. Future contracts on additional products were negotiated, and the manufacturing company became a preferred supplier to this customer.

This example shows that we must be ready to have difficult conversations, fix damaged relationships, and take responsibility. To see the opportunity when problems arise, we must listen to and accept criticism to learn. Many times, our ideas will be rejected. We may have to change ingrained habits and exhibit new behaviors. It often takes a high degree of collaboration and imagination. In other words, we must do what needs to be done to create the conditions under which opportunities can present themselves.

As we approach problems, it becomes clear that optimism is required. Churchill also said, "The pessimist sees difficulty in every opportunity; the optimist sees opportunity in every difficulty."

Takeaways: Problems Are Opportunities Dressed in Work Clothes

- All problems are opportunities; solving them adds value.
- Solving problems creates risk, and fear of failure is an inhibitor.
  - Reputational risk is not trying.
  - You learn nothing by not trying.
- It's not about working hard but about hard work. This involves:
  - change.
  - rising to the challenge, overcoming fear, and difficult decisions.
  - starting again after every failure.
  - being out of your "comfort zone."
  - difficult conversations.
  - fixing damaged relationships.
  - taking responsibility.
  - accepting criticism and dealing with rejection.
  - changing ingrained habits, learning new behaviors, and exhibiting optimism.
- The pessimist sees difficulty in every opportunity while the optimist sees opportunity in every difficulty (Churchill).

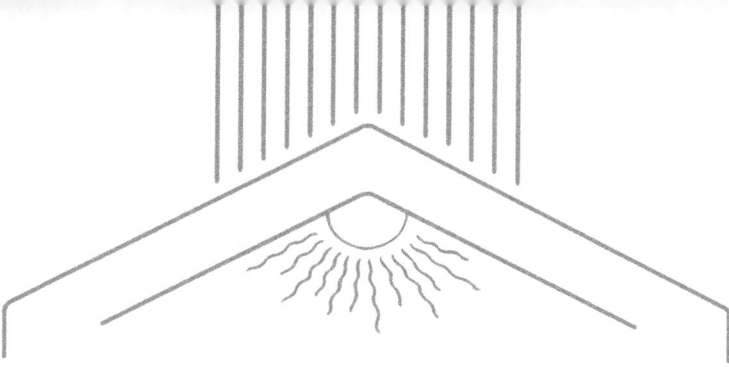

TOUCHSTONE #30

In Theory, There Is No Difference between Theory and Practice. In Practice, There Is

This Touchstone has been attributed separately to two vastly different people, Albert Einstein and Yogi Berra. Concrete evidence of either of them ever stating this has yet to be found. Notwithstanding, the message embodied here is helpful to all leaders. Theories and models often guide us to help make critical decisions, but we must also be mindful of their limitations.

Theories are models of an event or situation based on logic and simplifying assumptions. It is this simplification that makes the theory usable. The applicability of these simplifying assumptions limits the practical usefulness of the theory. Keeping these assumptions at the forefront of our thinking is essential when drawing conclusions from any theory or model (Solow, 2023).

Applying the theory to a practical situation requires experience and often empirical data to validate the theory, define its limitations, and interpret the results it provides properly. Hands-on experience is essential for putting the theory into practice. It is important to remember not to believe everything that comes out of a computer. Always be skeptical of the numbers and refer to the assumptions underpinning the model and their applicability to the situation at hand.

Those using scientific or engineering theoretical models are usually aware of the difference between theory and practice. But it must be considered in the business world as well. Business leaders must understand the limitations of the financial modeling used in evaluating different business activities. Again, we must remember that financial modeling is a theoretical treatment and an approximation of reality.

> Theories are models of an event or situation based on logic and simplifying assumptions.

The financial model's assumptions must be scrutinized when applying the model to a business situation. The assumptions behind investments must be scrutinized before making final decisions. Valuing companies and specific assets is subject to considerable theoretical shortcomings because models of future results must be included in the analysis.

Business strategy also relies on assumptions of the future of markets, customers, product demand, and many other aspects of the industry. The assumptions used to create the forecasts must be evaluated continuously, and adjustments must be made to align the strategy with our latest understanding of the business.

Takeaways: In Theory, There Is No Difference between Theory & Practice. In Practice, There Is

- Theories are models of reality that use simplifying assumptions.
    - It is this simplification that makes the theory usable.
    - These assumptions limit the applicability.
- To apply the theory to a practical situation requires experience or empirical data to supplement the limitations of the theory.
    - Hands-on experience is essential for putting theory into practice.
    - Don't believe everything that comes out of the computer.
    - Be skeptical of the numbers.
- Those using scientific or engineering theoretical models are usually well aware of the difference between theory and practice.
- Financial modeling is a theoretical treatment or approximation of reality.
    - The financial model's assumptions must be scrutinized when applying the model to a practical situation or business transaction.
    - Valuing companies and assets is subject to considerable theoretical shortcomings.

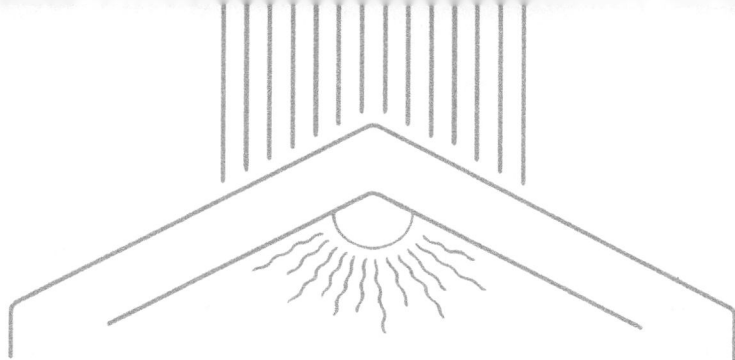

TOUCHSTONE #31

Forecasts Should Be Accurate; Targets Should Be Ambitious

This Touchstone triggers a considerable amount of challenge and debate. Some feel that forecasts should be developed such that, if targets are achieved, the forecast will become a reality. This approach will lead to relatively easy targets since people want to ensure the forecast is met. A more entrepreneurial approach treats forecasting and target setting as *related* but *different*.

Targets should be superior results that an organization desires to achieve. These targets are, therefore, a stretch from the status quo and an improvement from the present condition. The organization's members must develop the targets. All must buy into the fact that, while difficult, these targets are achievable. Also, we must realize that, by definition, an ambitious sales target cannot be simultaneously an unbiased estimate (Creelman, 2017).

On the other hand, forecasts estimate what is most likely to occur based on current data and marketing information. To prepare these forecasts, an unbiased viewpoint must be established to the extent possible. This is a challenging assignment for the execution team. Sound leadership from the top of the organization is essential.

The final review and approval of the forecast is best achieved if the decision-maker is not close to the preparation and adopts an outside view to weed out optimistic or pessimistic biases that may creep into the forecast.

Probing and questioning the assumptions used to prepare the forecast is the best way to ferret out these potential biases. It is especially important to achieve this outside view as a leader and final decision-maker when evaluating major business investments that may be part of the business plan. This is essential to eliminate the many different biases that creep into the development of the team's business proposal (Kahneman et al., 2011a and Kahneman, 2011b). Therefore, targets are set by *looking at* what is *possible*, while forecasts are based on what is *most likely*.

> Targets should be superior results that an organization desires to achieve.

The objective, or unbiased, forecast is a useful tool to guide a company to achieve its stretch targets. When we compare the forecast and the targets, there will be a gap in certain performance measures. As we examine these gaps and the assumptions that cause them, we will develop ideas and actions to close them over time. Thus, it will become much more obvious where to address improvements in the company's systems, operations, and cost structure.

The use of rolling forecasts makes the forecasting tool even more effective. Rolling forecasts always look forward to the same period. So, if we use a quarterly approach, as one quarter finishes, we add an additional quarter to the updated forecast future. Therefore, we are not just focused on year-end results but are always looking forward at least twelve months.

A more modern approach to forecasting goes a step further. Dynamic forecasting builds upon rolling forecasts by updating the forecast when something material happens and adjusting the look-forward period as far ahead as relevant for the specific business. Thus, the forecast period will vary business by business.

Key performance indicators (KPIs) or other metrics must be set properly. The forecast and targets must be aligned with these KPIs. This approach will provide a methodology to track progress as well as provide direction to achieve the desired outcome of achieving the targets. Setting the correct KPIs is essential (Calzon, 2022).

Takeaways: Forecasts Should Be Accurate; Targets Should Be Ambitious

- The Difference Between Forecasts and Targets:
    - A *target* is a superior result that the organization desires to achieve. It is usually a stretch from the status quo and an improvement from the present condition.
    - A *forecast* is an estimate of what most likely will occur based on current data and information.
    - Forecasts should be periodically updated to see if we can put the business on track to achieve the targets.
    - Rolling forecasts and dynamic forecasting are helpful tools.
- An ambitious sales target cannot be simultaneously an unbiased estimate.
- The decision-maker must adopt an outside view to expose optimistic biases.
- All forecasts are wrong; some forecasts are useful.
- A KPI methodology is very useful to gauge progress toward achieving targets and updating rolling forecasts.

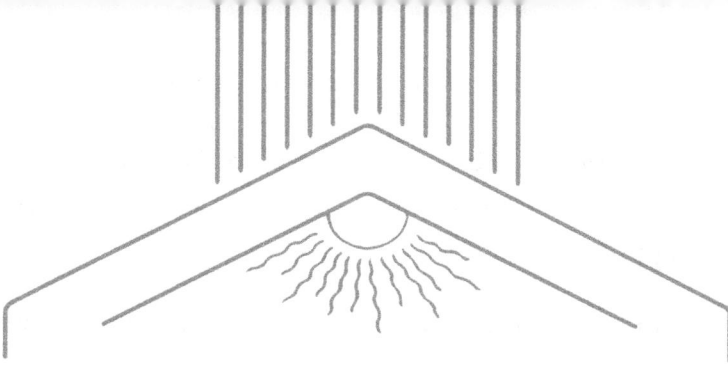

TOUCHSTONE #32

Focus on Results and People, Not Methods

Delivering meaningful results creates value. Focusing on the results and metrics that matter to drive business value is important.

Our processes are important, but the process is the tool; the results create value. This thinking is not universal. Some believe that the results will naturally come if you get the right processes in place. I have not found this to be true. If the goals are different from the objective of our work, the results achieved may not be meaningful to drive the value of the business.

Of course, we need good processes to achieve results. Process centers and process owners are important to maintain strong operations compliant with internal standards, process improvement initiatives, and ever-changing external regulatory requirements. However, unnecessary or "gold-plated" processes are apt to be developed without keeping the team's eyes on the results. This is because working on processes is open-ended. One can always make them better. Focusing on results will drive the business to fix those processes inhibiting achieving the desired results.

The best way to become results-focused is to develop, track, and review metrics. The following guidelines help drive a results-oriented culture:

- Create metrics required for effective oversight of the business.

- Review metrics regularly as they are updated.

- Act when results trend in the wrong direction or data don't make sense.

- Don't "nag" or focus on the small things when results are good.

- Take measures to minimize "fake" results.

Having a results-focused approach also provides an easier path for a fast-growing company. A company with a results orientation and managing by exception typically requires fewer management resources for the same outcomes. This reduces the investment needed for growth and allows a more rapid transition to a larger organization.

Furthermore, focusing on results helps employees know how their success will be measured and helps build morale. This is where management skills and interpersonal skills merge. Research shows (Zenger and Folkman, 2009) that great leaders possess both a results orientation together with strong social and people skills. This research was a result of over 60,000 interviews. It showed that leaders strong in results orientation alone had only a 14 percent chance of being seen as great leaders. Leaders with strong social skills but needing more results orientation were seen as great leaders only 12 percent of the time. A leader with strong social

Delivering meaningful results creates value.

skills coupled with a strong results orientation, however, has a 72 percent chance of being considered a great leader.

Neurological research (Lieberman, 2013a, 2013b) attempts to understand and explain why it is so difficult for leaders to possess these two sets of skills simultaneously. There are distinct regions of the brain that control the analytical function and the social interaction function. Lieberman's research demonstrates that when one of these regions got more active, the other region became quieter. Therefore, engaging in analytical thinking makes it harder to engage in social thinking and vice versa.

Great leaders must learn how to quickly switch from one type of thinking to the other as the need arises and recognize *when* the switch is necessary.

Takeaways: Focus on Results and People, Not Methods

- Create value by delivering results and outcomes.
    - Process is important, but process is the tool, not the value creation.
    - We need good processes and methods to achieve results.
    - Without keeping the team's eye on the result, unnecessary or "gold-plated" processes may be developed.
    - Focusing on results will drive you to fix those processes required to achieve the results.
- Take specific steps to become results oriented:
    - Create metrics required for effective oversight of your business.
    - Review metrics regularly as they are updated.
    - Act when results trend in the wrong direction or data don't make sense.
    - Don't "nag" or focus on the small things when results are good.
    - Take measures to minimize "fake" results.
- Develop scalability by focusing on results.
- Focus on results, as this builds morale and helps employees know how their success will be measured.

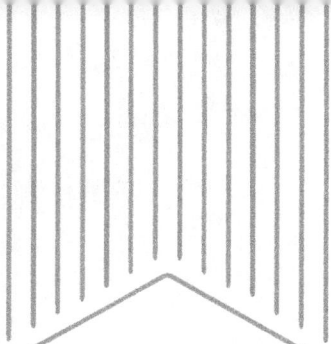

PART 4

Strategy and Alignment

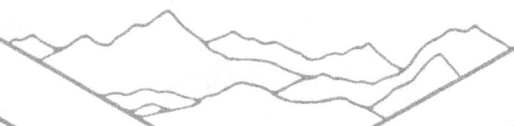

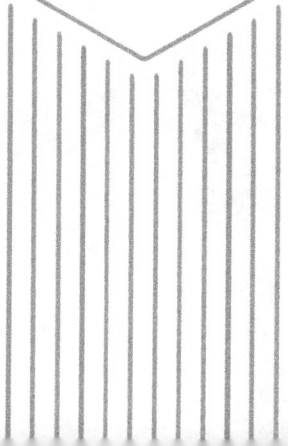

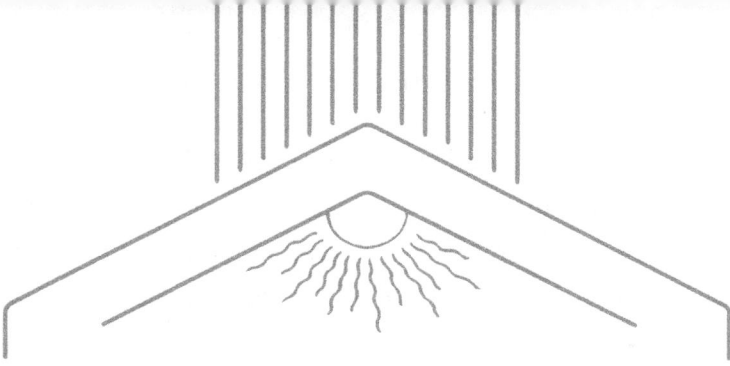

TOUCHSTONE #33

Strategy Is about Deliberately Choosing to Be Different

The foundations of business strategy and understanding of competition, including this Touchstone, are embodied in the works of Michael Porter (Porter, 1987, 1996, 2009). Building on this body of work, we find the most direct definition: *business strategy is a company's unique way of sustainable value creation* (Kraaijenbrink, 2019).

As Porter so clearly points out, uniquely creating value is the driver of competitive success. Therefore, they compete to be unique. Don't compete to be the best at an activity. You must change the paradigm and be different from your rivals. In sports, there is only one winner because the rules are fixed.

In business, we are focused on meeting many customers' needs. This leads to companies focusing on different needs and specializing so that multiple winners can coexist and thrive in various industries. As opposed to sports, the engagement rules are not fixed in business. A company can tailor its business model to maintain a competitive advantage. So, business competition should not be about *beating* your competitors but *competing* with them for profits. Sometimes, you can collaborate with a competitor to make more profit together than you would alone.

When companies employ a war strategy with their competitors, customer benefits are not increased, and customers can be negatively affected. There are several examples: GM and Ford went to war with the Japanese in the late 1970s and early 1980s. The large airlines tried to beat Southwest Airlines with low-cost flights but failed miserably. Steve Jobs and Apple declared war on Google. They pledged to destroy Android with an inferior map, which infuriated Apple customers and caused Jobs's successor to apologize and bear severe criticism. Making a strategy about the competition can be quite destructive, whereas strategies that focus on the customer continue to provide a true competitive advantage.

> When companies employ a war strategy with their competitors, customer benefits are not increased, and customers can be negatively affected.

The industry structure determines the average profitability of the businesses in that particular industry. A company's relative position within its industry determines whether its profits are above or below the industry average. A company with a competitive advantage can maintain a higher relative price, operate at a lower relative cost, or both. Therefore, a company with a true competitive advantage will be sustainably more profitable than the industry average.

A good place to start is applying Porter's Five Forces to assess an industry and form a business strategy. This will define the industry's structure, give insight into the average economics of the industry, and point to areas where you can differentiate your business to increase its profitability. The Five Forces are as follows:

- Threat of New Entrants

- Supplier Power

- Buyer Power

- Threat of Substitutions

- Rivalry among Competitors

Generally, the stronger the forces, the less profitable the industry or business area is. To analyze the industry properly, defining the boundaries in both product and geographic scope is necessary. When comparing different business lines, Porter's rule is that if differences are in more than one force, or the difference in one force is very large, you are likely dealing with business lines that each need a separate strategy.

An in-depth five forces analysis not only assesses the attractiveness of an industry or business area but also provides insight into how you can position your business to be more competitive and vie for a greater share of the industry's profits.

Takeaways: Strategy Is about Deliberately Choosing to Be Different

- Competing to be the best at an activity doesn't work in the long run.
- Operational effectiveness is not a strategy.
- You must be unique and create superior value for customers and investors to maintain a competitive advantage.
- Competitive advantage is a sustainable difference in delivering value, not winning a war with competitors.
- Strategy must link to the company's financial performance.
- Industry structure determines average profitability.
    - Porter's Five Forces provide an analysis of the industry structure.
    - A company's competitive advantage determines whether profits are above or below the average in an industry.
- Value chain differentiation will drive a company's competitive advantage.
- A concrete strategy identifies a unique position that provides a sustainable advantage.

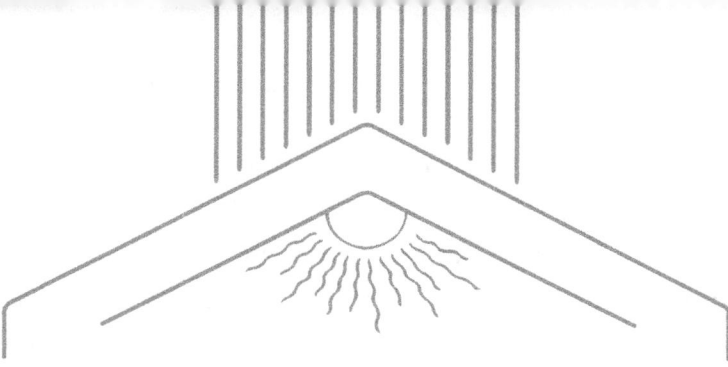

TOUCHSTONE #34

The Essence of Strategy Is Choosing What Not to Do

As a company develops a strategy that will differentiate itself, it becomes important to define which customers will be served, which needs will be served, and how to do this by creating value. This must also be done while maintaining profitability to provide a return on the investments made and planned to be made in the company. A true strategy encompasses the whole of the business.

Porter's work addresses how to develop and evaluate business strategy. It is another example of why focus is so important across the board. Porter has developed five tests of every good strategy (Magretta, 2012). These can be listed as follows:

- *A distinctive value proposition*: Businesses must be different from their rivals, with an external focus on customers and the demand side of the business. Also, there is a focus on profitability.

- *A tailored value chain*: Businesses must perform different activities or the same activities differently. This includes internal focus on the supply side of the business and on creating value that can provide a "hook" that cannot be easily imitated.

- *Trade-offs, the linchpin*: Businesses cannot make choices that are incompatible with one another. They must choose what not to do and be particularly clear about it. They must accept their limits. Also, trade-offs are challenging to match or neutralize by the competition. In addition, trade-offs provide grounds for customer segmentation.

- *Fit across the value chain, the differentiator*: Businesses must connect activities in the value chain to create differentiation. This is an interdependent connection that increases value generation. Fit reduces the ability of competitors to copy or imitate the strategy by creating obstacles for would-be imitators.

- *Continuity over time, the enabler*: Businesses must maintain stability at the core of the strategy. This continuity reinforces identity and helps customers, suppliers, and other partners solidify company confidence. It provides time for the strategy to mature and evolve. Also, continuity guides when improvements or changes need to be made.

These tests of a strategy make it clear that a company cannot be all things to all people. As you think about choosing what not to do, one of the more difficult choices has to do with customers. At first, one may think that all customers who desire your products or services will benefit your business. However, as you think deeper into this, it becomes clear that certain customer orders or operating methods need to fit your differentiation strategy. Therefore, they may distract from your ability to perform in the long run. Also, customers have different needs. Customer segmentation is a significant part of choosing what not to do and is important in differentiating your business from the competition.

It is always tempting to deviate from the strategy when presented with a highly attractive business opportunity inconsistent with the strategic direction. But, pursuing it can be destructive in the long run as resources get diverted to a profitable venture, causing the inability to respond to an opportunity in the business strategy's sweet spot. That is not to say we won't pick up a "golden nugget" we see by the road, but we shouldn't go off the road to look for it.

As we focus on strategy, it becomes clear that there are three fundamental ways to create value. We must provide a superior product, a superior price, or a superior solution. Furthermore, it becomes evident that we can be truly superior at only one.

Finally, leaders must remain aware of changes in the business environment and adapt to the ever-changing world (Covey, 1992). This does not mean that the strategy needs to change, but the systems and processes to implement the strategy may need to be updated. In extreme cases, some fundamental changes in strategic direction may be required.

Takeaways: The Essence of Strategy Is Choosing What Not To Do

- A true strategy encompasses the whole of the business.
- We should remember Porter's five tests of every good strategy:
  - a distinctive value proposition
  - a tailored value chain
  - trade-offs different from rivals, the linchpin
  - fit across the value chain, the differentiator
  - continuity over time, the enabler
- A company cannot be all things to all people.
  - Customer segmentation is an important consideration.
- There are three fundamental ways to create value:
  - superior product
  - superior price
  - superior solution
- Focus is the key.

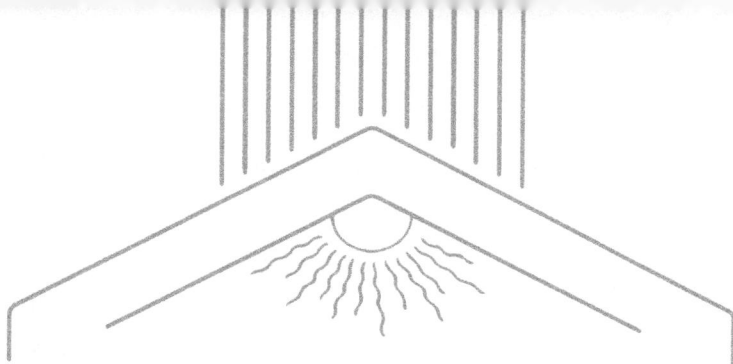

TOUCHSTONE #35

If You Can't Fix It, Feature It

This axiom has long been one of the best tools in the industry used to reposition liabilities as assets and change negative perceptions into positive ones.

Certain unavoidable negative situations or conditions are often encountered as part of doing business. These may even threaten a company's reputation or give customers or investors pause. Sometimes, they are simply the weaknesses embedded in the business. These negative situations, however, are very often not truly detrimental to your delivering products or providing services in the long run. Therefore, there is a natural tendency to distract others from the negative issue or avoid discussing it. Often, a smarter solution is to turn this liability into an asset. It also can become a point of differentiation from the competition.

So, it is often better to lead with the negative perception and disarm your detractors. Trial lawyers consistently use this approach in defending their clients' history (Gesmer, 2011). They lead with this before the prosecution can bring it up. The defense lawyer then demonstrates why this prior past has made their client now a better person.

If they wait for the prosecution to bring this up, the jury will think they were trying to hide this.

It is similar to business. If it cannot be fixed near term, lead with it. In this context, identify or perceive weaknesses in marketing the company, and look at them through the lens of turning them into assets that can be presented in a positive sense. There are a few classic examples:

If it cannot be fixed near term, lead with it.

- In the 1960s, Avis was the clear second car rental agency in fierce competition to the market leader Hertz. Realizing they could not become first, Avis led with this fact and came up with the pitch, "When you're only No. 2, you try harder." The new tagline aimed to promote their superior service. The "We Try Harder" ads almost instantly impacted profits and increased market share. The perceived weakness of being number two was turned into an asset.

- There was likely a concern that the Smucker's jellies and jams business in the United States would have a branding problem. While the family wanted to maintain the recipes under the Smucker's name, they faced the dilemma of how to proceed. Again, instead of considering this a liability, the family adopted the powerful slogan, "With a name like Smucker's, it has to be good" (Engelberg, 2005).

- The nine-hole golf courses that began springing up were considered somewhat inferior. Then, someone got the idea to market them as executive courses. This suggests that their players are very important and much too busy to have the time to play eighteen holes.

One approach to finding those liabilities that may be suitable to feature as potential assets is to examine what our marketing efforts are trying to deflect or hide. By using this self-examining method, companies have found several approaches to overcome their liabilities.

Takeaways: If You Can't Fix It, Feature It

- Often, negative situations are unavoidable. But they can be assets.
  - Instead of hiding them, lead with them.
  - Look at believed weaknesses from a fresh viewpoint.
  - Perceived negatives can be competitive differentiators.
- In 1962, Avis featured that they were number two and "tried harder."
- "With a name like Smucker's, you've got to be good."
- If you are selling fried food, don't pretend like it is healthy.
- Nine-hole golf courses are featured as executive courses.
- If you can't fix it, then fix it. However, if you can't fix it, then feature it.
- Turn those things, which you think are your liabilities, into assets.
- What do we assume are liabilities? What does our program currently "hide"?

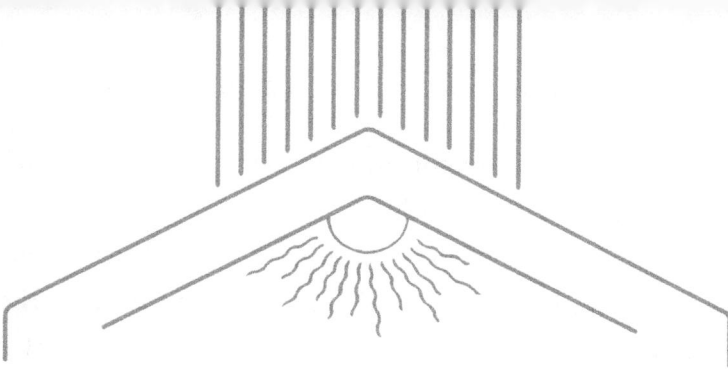

TOUCHSTONE #36

Focus on What's Strategically Best; Outsource the Rest

Traditionally, many companies focus on "core competencies" as they decide what to perform in-house versus outsourcing. This approach, however, while important, can inhibit a company from being as competitive as it could be. Porter proposes that in addition to the business's core capabilities, it is important to look at the entire value chain and determine which activities can be tailored to add value from a strategic fit perspective.

Activities determined to be nonessential to the strategy or generic can be safely outsourced. Tailored ones provide unique competitive value and should be kept in-house or brought in-house if currently outsourced. It is important to retain control of those tailored activities to maintain the best competitive advantage.

As new technologies emerge and are applied to a company's products, it is the ideal time to reexamine the outsourcing strategy. For example, consider the electric vehicle (EV). As carmakers continue investing in EVs, we see the emerging debate of direct outsourcing of lithium-ion batteries versus other more strategic approaches. The

EV battery is a critical component from many respects: cost, weight, efficiency, reliability, and availability.

The input raw materials (e.g., lithium and cobalt) are in rare supply, and countries are vying to control these materials. The EV manufacturer that develops a battery strategy that gives them a superior competitive advantage will become the leader and generate the best return on their invested capital. So, when new technologies enter your industry, review your outsourcing strategy to create a competitive advantage.

The demand by consumers for more natural products, especially in foods, beverages, and cosmetics, also drives manufacturers to a unique make-versus-buy strategy. To become truly natural products, all traditionally synthetic ingredients used in these products must be replaced by natural ingredients and processed without chemicals. Synthetic ingredients are made in chemical facilities to very tight specifications and are well controlled.

Activities determined to be nonessential to the strategy or generic can be safely outsourced.

Natural products (and ingredients) are often based on farm products and can vary widely based on geography, soil composition, weather conditions, and other external factors. This opens the door for different strategic approaches to how or whether to outsource raw materials for natural products. Exclusive partnerships and further vertical integration become viable options to attain a competitive advantage. So, as market demands change, it is important to use them to improve a company's competitive advantage.

When we entered the twenty-first century, some large U.S. and European pharmaceutical companies started changing their outsourcing policies to acquire materials from India and China. This provided them with much lower pricing on the ingredients. This lowered the cost of goods but needed to be more strategic as the rest of the companies followed suit, and no competitive advantage was achieved.

This was not truly a tailoring of their value chain since it was so easily imitated. Meanwhile, many traditional Western suppliers went out of business or removed capacity. Some redirected their assets to other industries. Over time, however, the pharmaceutical companies found many areas for improvement in this supply chain. Some Eastern suppliers got into regulatory problems, causing program delays and disruptions.

Government issues within China caused delays as well. Total savings from this outsourcing move were less than expected. Two decades later, the pandemic caused ruptures in the complex supply chains. Now, pharma companies are returning to Western suppliers but need more capability in the West to manufacture the starting materials. Years ago, a strategic approach to outsourcing would have given a few companies a competitive advantage.

These examples show that tailoring the value chain when we see technological changes, changes in customer sentiment, or changes in global conditions can be a way for a company to avoid major impacts on the business and maintain a competitive advantage.

Sometimes, we see a way to tailor the value chain, but the in-house capability to address this tailoring doesn't exist. One way to address this is through a focused tuck-in acquisition. Acquiring a small company with the expertise needed is a very rapid way to develop the tailoring needed. Another way is to license the technology needed.

Takeaways: Focus on What's Strategically Best; Outsource the Rest

- Outsourcing must be aligned with the value chain strategy's tailoring, trade-offs, and fit.
- Ask which activities are generic and which can be tailored to strategy.
- We must be best in the critical value adders to the business.
- Outsourcing on partnering should be in nonessential or generic areas that don't create a true differentiation. A manufacturing company may want to outsource some "back-office" activities.
- Smaller, tuck-in acquisitions can help fill the value chain with tailored activities.
- Licensing technology or capability can also be a way to tailor your value chain.
- There are still those strategists who promote total vertical integration.
    - We are seeing a move back to more vertical integration through acquisitions.
    - This is a very tricky area today.
- Is outsourcing critical activities true partnering? Does this approach reduce our competitiveness over the long run?

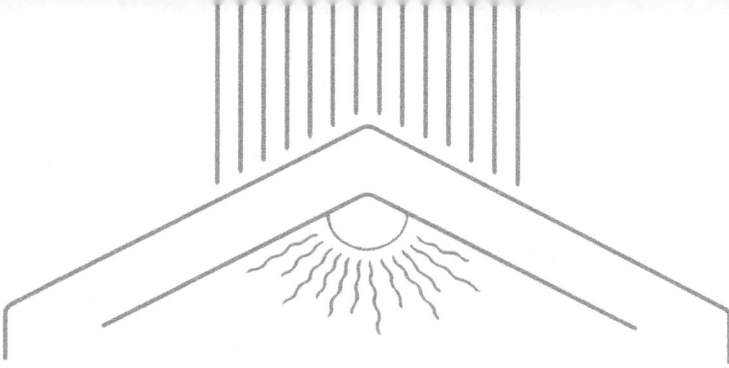

TOUCHSTONE #37

Feed Opportunities; Starve Problems

Only opportunities will lead to growth and success. Growing a company, therefore, requires developing and capitalizing on business opportunities (Drucker, 1993). Many companies, however, focus on their weaknesses and problem areas while putting opportunities on the "back burner."

This thinking can pervade the culture of the business, causing a severe imbalance in the workforce's perceived priorities. Have you ever run into an employee who purposely finds a simple problem that could be solved in a few hours or, at most, a few days and then blows it out of proportion to be a major threat to the well-being of the company? The employee then becomes the hero and puts the issue to rest through a complicated problem-solving route, gaining the attention of upper management and sometimes even an award. Such activity feeds the problem and diverts valuable time and resources from pursuing other opportunities that can help grow the business.

Of course, critical problems need to be solved to preserve the performance and reputation of the company but not at the expense of the opportunities. Also, there tend to be very few critical problems. A good rule is that if the problem threatens the strategy and the company's mission, it needs to be dealt with quickly and without fanfare. Other issues can be handled over time in a prioritized fashion without depleting the organization's resources. Many solutions can be outsourced, leaving company assets to work on growth opportunities. Refraining from allowing people to work a problem into a career is important.

Everyday problems are like weeds in a garden (Catlette and Hadden, 2013). You don't want to ignore them or give them much time and attention. Get rid of them carefully, but don't fertilize, water, or encourage them to grow.

Therefore, applying your most talented staff to the opportunities rather than the problems is important. However, Drucker's work shows that there is a tendency for companies to do the opposite and assign the best people to problems rather than growth opportunities. It is human nature to focus on weaknesses and try to fix them. It takes strategic vision and courage to do the opposite. This is a sign of true leadership. In *Good to Great* (Collins, 2001) and the companion monograph, *Turning the Flywheel* (Collins, 2019), the excellent research shows that the companies that moved from good to great created a culture of assigning their best people to their most promising opportunities. It is important to grasp this concept. Managing your problems can make you a good company, but great companies focus on building and capitalizing upon opportunities.

> Only opportunities will lead to growth and success.

An important exception exists when assigning one of your most talented personnel to a problem area is warranted. That is when you believe that the problem area can be turned into a true opportunity and that there is a reasonable, or even high, probability of achieving that outcome. You must, however, get this assessment of the probability of success correct. It is important to understand the industry and the market to ensure this is the right move. If true, it can be extremely rewarding.

Takeaways: Feed Opportunities; Starve Problems

- Only opportunities will lead to growth.
- Time, talents, and treasure are better spent on those tasks that offer growth potential.
- Focus your best people on opportunities.
- Turn perceived problems into opportunities.
- Real problems that threaten to destroy your strategy must be eliminated quickly without fanfare.
- Do not feed or encourage these problems in any way.

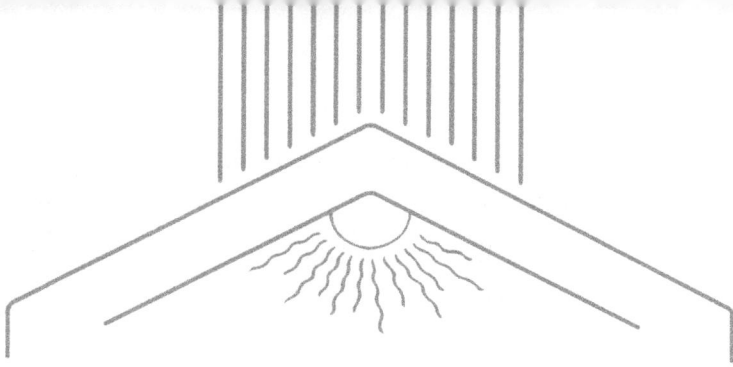

TOUCHSTONE #38

Bad News Is Not like Good Wine; It Doesn't Get Better with Age

A company must address its challenges head-on.

When there is bad news, and something goes seriously wrong, the mature leader will face this, understand it, and do what is necessary to rectify the situation in a timely manner, regardless of the personal cost or the cost to the company. Weak leaders often wait to act in these situations, hoping to find a more graceful way out or even expecting the problem to be resolved without subjecting themselves and the company to public embarrassment or legal liability.

These leaders must realize that the problems invariably compound and become more severe and expensive. If the problem is a safety issue, people can become harmed or even die while the company is trying to figure out how to evade public scrutiny. Cover-ups can happen at all levels within the company, and it is the job of the leader and the leadership team to ensure that this behavior is uncovered and the guilty parties are dismissed.

There have been numerous instances where companies caused severe and sometimes fatal situations by not revealing issues and delaying or concealing their solution. In many cases, high-ranking individuals falsified records to evade reporting the problem. If they had acknowledged the problem and recalled the products promptly, they could have saved lives, time, and money for everyone. The following are a few examples.

TAKATA AUTOMOBILE AIRBAGS

In the late 1990s, a new generation of automobile airbags was introduced to the industry. These new airbag designs replaced the sodium azide used in earlier models with nitrate-based, less toxic chemicals. Takata was one of the first companies to bring these new airbags to the market, supplying them to Honda. Takata was the only airbag supplier to use ammonium nitrate to replace sodium azide, while others used guanidine nitrate. Takata was successful in selling their airbags to most of the other major car manufacturers. However, over-pressurizations of the Takata airbags started to occur in 2004–2005, projecting metal from the airbag inflator at high speeds and causing injuries and, in some cases, fatalities. Although a series of limited recalls were conducted, the root cause of the failures was never exposed.

It was later discovered that the Takata airbags had this problem because, as ammonium nitrate aged, it absorbed moisture, causing the over-pressurization problem primarily in high-humidity locations. However, no one in charge wanted to accept this "bad news" and find a permanent solution to fix the problem. Apparently, Takata management knew the extent and the cause of the problem but covered it up, presumably because airbags were a major source of their income. Even with repeated consumer injuries and deaths, Takata senior management continued to withhold the actual airbag test data from the public.

Finally, Takata released the information and admitted that it defrauded car manufacturers and customers for nearly two decades by manipulating test data. After this, major settlements were reached.

ASBESTOS COVER-UP

The health risks of working with asbestos were known for a very long time. In fact, Pliny the Elder, circa 100 AD, wrote of the respiratory diseases of the slaves who were mining asbestos. The medical profession established links between asbestos fiber particle inhalation and serious respiratory illnesses as early as the 1930s.

Doctors made warnings to companies dealing with asbestos, but these companies ignored their warnings. One of the most infamous cases was that of the Johns Manville company. Their executives edited insurance company reports regarding their employees, ignored advice to place warning labels on asbestos products, and tacitly held to a policy not to act on asbestos issues and not disclose certain medical information to employees (Richards, 1978).

Johns Manville executives solved complaints quietly through compensation settlements, which forced employees not to disclose any details, including the cause of respiratory illnesses. As more and more people became ill from asbestos, massive cover-ups were exposed (Simmons, 2013). This resulted in many companies going bankrupt.

VOLKSWAGEN EMISSIONS AND FUEL MILEAGE REPORTS

From 2005 to 2015, Volkswagen (VW) claimed that their diesel passenger cars were environmentally friendly. However, as emissions standards became more stringent, VW struggled to meet them. To address this issue, VW developed software that would align with the Environmental Protection Agency's (EPA) emissions test standards. This allowed the diesel engines to pass the tests. However, the software settings also reduced the car's mileage and power.

To avoid disappointing consumers, VW implemented a separate software mode for normal driving that restored power but no longer met the emissions standards. This meant that there was a test mode to satisfy the EPA and a separate, undisclosed mode for regular driving. After an investigation, VW admitted to cheating and settled with consumers for almost $15 billion.

Unfortunately, VW did not learn from this incident. Several years later, they admitted to cheating again, this time with gasoline-powered cars that were supposed to meet fuel economy standards. The software in these cars would shift gears in a manner that optimized fuel economy during EPA tests but not during actual driving conditions. As a result, consumers were getting lower fuel efficiency than they were promised. The consumers sued, and VW settled with them.

FROZEN COKE MARKETING COVER-UP

With beverage sales waning, in 2000, the Coca-Cola company was planning to launch a Frozen Coke product. They entered into an agreement with Burger King to roll out a nationwide promotion for this novel product. The agreement to proceed with the rollout was predicated on a successful pilot marketing test in the Richmond, Virginia, area.

This test offered a free coupon for a Frozen Coke to customers who purchased a value meal at Burger King. The marketing test was not going well. Those in charge of this test did not want to bring the "bad news" back to the headquarters, as it may have killed the nation-wide rollout. So, they rigged the test by paying a Virginia resident $10,000 to buy Burger King value meals for hundreds of kids, thus biasing the results in their favor (Day, 2003).

> A culture where no bad news is wanted cannot be tolerated.

At the same time, Coca-Cola was involved in an unrelated employee lawsuit. The opponents in this lawsuit uncovered and made public the rigged tests as part of their process. Burger King saw this and threatened to pull out of their agreement. This was eventually resolved, but Coca-Cola's reputation was damaged.

CONCLUSION

These examples are ones that have been highly publicized because of the public nature of their impact. They also show that it is always best to own up to a bad situation and get it behind you, no matter how painful in the near term. Unfortunately, many acts of not reporting bad news go unobserved within many companies. If this happens, this cultural issue must be corrected for a company to thrive. Situations that seem insignificant at the outset can grow into major problems if not handled.

A culture where no bad news is wanted cannot be tolerated. Silence is often caused by fear of speaking up, fear of being tagged as a troublemaker by management, or even fear of being ridiculed by peers and subordinates. One way to help shift the culture is to reward those who speak up, especially in situations where it is risky to do so.

We had a situation where some rust particles were found in a drum of a pharmaceutical chemical product. Finding the source of this in a chemical plant is a very serious and costly process. After explaining the problem to the manufacturing crew and how we would have to shut the plant down for, perhaps, weeks, one chemical operator came forward. He was the cause of this because he accidentally dropped a rusty part into the drum before the drum being filled.

Knowing that the rust did not come from the processing saved much time and money. Instead of punishing the offender, we rewarded him with gift cards for coming forward in front of his peers. This inspired the whole manufacturing team to be vigilant and report issues as soon as they occurred.

Often, people look at whether an action is *legal* rather than whether an action is the *proper* thing to do. They may present you with a clever approach to create an advantage for the company that pushes the ethical boundaries. When you challenge them, you often hear, "Well, it is legal." This is a good time to use the *Wall Street Journal* (*WSJ*) Test. Ask the employee if they would be comfortable if their creative scheme were printed on the front page of the *WSJ*. Pondering that question will wake them up to the fact that their idea will damage them and the company.

Takeaways: Bad News Is Not like Good Wine; It Doesn't Get Better With Age

- A company must address its challenges head-on.
- It is always the cover-up that becomes the big problem.
- It's always best to own up to a bad situation and get it behind you.
- You cannot tolerate a culture where "no bad news is wanted" by the leadership.
- We must battle against fear and silence.
- Reward those who report bad news despite the risk to themselves.
- Create a culture of acceptance when reporting bad news.
- Can what you are doing pass the " *Wall Street Journal* Test"? If it is on the front page of the *WSJ*, will you be okay with it?

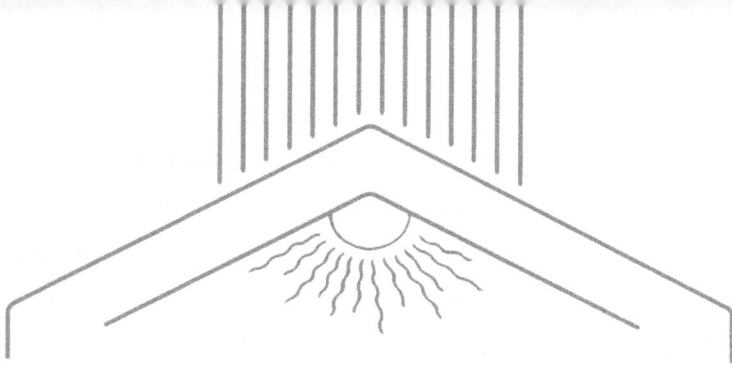

TOUCHSTONE #39

Always Keep Time on Your Side

When involved in a business transaction, one of the worst situations you can encounter is to be forced to complete the transaction because of time constraints. Sometimes, this is unavoidable, but most times, good planning, combined with realistic time parameters, can avoid such situations.

This Touchstone does not refer to traditional time management, that is, the efficient use of time. Traditional time management, which is very important, is covered in many project management teachings. Here, the emphasis is on the overall vision of how a very critical transaction will play out and how the leader needs to ensure that the proper actions are undertaken early enough in the process so that there is no undue pressure to complete the transaction before all aspects are considered. You don't want lack of time to be the cause of making a serious error.

A way to avoid getting into a major time crunch is to plan when and how to execute the changes necessary. To exemplify this, think of someone in a kayak moving down the rapids that may be fraught with significant obstacles that are initially out of sight. As the kayak progresses, they see rocks and tree trunks in the distance. Immediately, they must gauge how fast they are moving and what turns are necessary to avoid hitting the obstacles. Then, when and how to maneuver becomes critical because of the speed. If the maneuvers are started too late, they cannot make the proper correction to avoid a disaster. Also, it will be prudent to maneuver even earlier than necessary.

Fundamentally, looking ahead is the best way to keep time on your side. Look ahead at what may be coming at you. A tough negotiation? A difficult phase of a significant project? A difficult personnel action? Restructuring the organization? Succession planning? Whatever it is, see it coming and plan. Start planning specific actions in advance so that there is time to execute the entire transaction or project to your satisfaction, and you are not pushed into doing something because of time constraints.

> Looking ahead is the best way to keep time on your side.

Schedule interference with the quality of your actions or decisions is also a problem when time is not on your side. It is especially important to preserve quality, as that is how most companies are judged in the long run. Some people take issue with this approach in negotiations where they feel they have significant leverage. They purposely try to put the other side in the negotiation under serious time pressure. Most times, this doesn't work and even backfires, and the deal never happens.

A good negotiator always considers no deal as an option.

Takeaways: Always Keep Time on Your Side

- We are not referring to "time management" in the traditional sense.
- We are referring to adequate planning in advance so that you are not time-constrained on significant business transactions.
- Identify achievable expectations when negotiating parameters for a project or contract.
- Plan for the unknowns.
- Try to eliminate schedule interference with the quality of your decisions, especially in negotiations of all types.

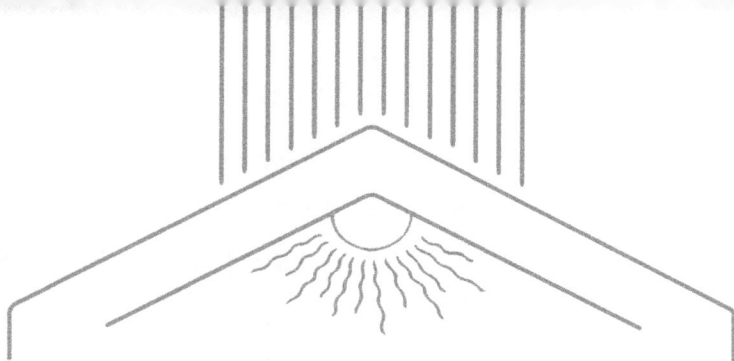

TOUCHSTONE #40

Maintain Strategic Continuity; Don't Keep Pulling Up the Flowers to See If the Roots Are Healthy

Patience. Patience. Patience.

If you have a good strategy, give it time to work. A good strategy is based on the fact that your customers and their needs are enduring. Therefore, gestation time is important to make your unique value proposition work. A good strategy should not be abandoned for small, near-term disappointments.

As we discussed previously, one of Porter's primary tests of a strategy is continuity. If the core of your strategy does not have stability and endurance, it will not survive, and you will need to repair or replace it. For a good strategy, however, there are several reasons why it is important to give it time to work:

- *Reason 1: To preserve the company's brand and identity*: It is important to convince customers that the company has a solid foundation. Continuity helps build customer relationships. Customers will be wary of providing long-term agreements if you are seen as constantly changing your strategic direction.

- *Reason 2: To allow building unique capabilities*: Continuity gives the company time to drive improvements and capabilities unique to its core strategy, constantly improving its competitive advantage.

- *Reason 3: To help suppliers and partners contribute*: Aligning the supply chain and all contributing outside parties with the strategy will improve the competitive advantage of the business. With a stable and constant strategy, the supply chain can be continually improved and tailored toward optimization.

Strategic continuity does not mean a company should stand still (Magretta, 2012). If the core value proposition continues to be valid, then there should be significant imaginative ways to improve the delivery of the basic value proposition. Constantly improving or even reinventing your methods remains the same fundamental strategy.

> A good strategy is based on the fact that your customers and their needs are enduring.

One example of long-term strategic continuity is Reuters. Paul Reuter saw a need for timely delivery of financial information, and that speed of delivery of this information would provide value to investors. In 1850, he used carrier pigeons to speed up the process. Throughout the years came the telegraph, teletype, telephone, and now the internet. Today, Reuters looks much different than in 1850, but the fundamental strategic value proposition hasn't changed, delivering rapid information to the financial markets and investors.

Walmart is another example of long-term continuity within a vastly changing business environment. Walmart opened in 1962, serving as a discount retailer of a segment of branded products to underserved, smaller communities. Today, it serves retail markets of all sizes with many product categories, including groceries. The technology of delivering these discounted products has changed drastically also. The fundamental value proposition, however, has stayed the same: deliver branded products at low prices.

Continuity of direction provides guidance about what's important to value creation and which marketplace or technology changes will affect your business and which changes will have no effect. Without a solid strategy, anything that changes may be important; you have no way of knowing. Having a concrete strategy grounded in the continuity of direction is extremely important during periods of marketplace and industry uncertainty. This will help guard a company against following the latest business trends or programs that may not benefit the company.

Takeaways: Maintain Strategic Continuity; Don't Keep Pulling Up the Flowers to See If the Roots Are Healthy

- A good strategy should not be changed for small, near-term disappointments.
  - Good strategies need time to work.
  - Changes in the industry and marketplace need to be assessed carefully before changing strategy.
- Patience, with follow-up, is essential.
  - Focus on things at the edge of your circle of influence.
  - Ensure the strategy is well thought out.
- Continuity provides a brand identity for customers, fosters internal improvements, and gives suppliers time to tailor their contribution.
- Make modifications as dictated by changes in the marketplace. Continuity gives the ability to adapt.

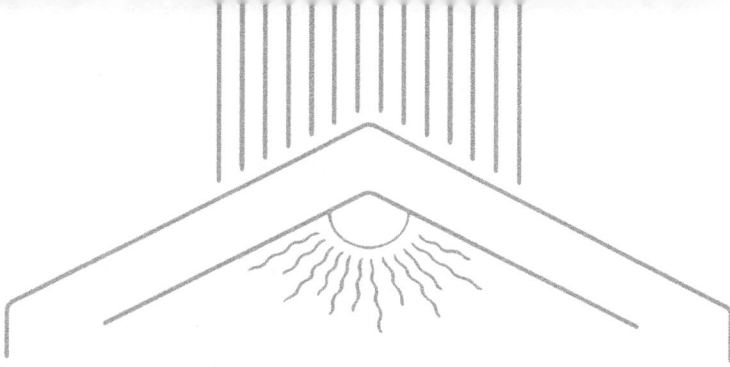

TOUCHSTONE # 41

Stop Doubling Down on Your Losing Strategy

There are times when the current business strategy becomes ineffective, and therefore, it is time to make a major shift (Magretta, 2012). This decision must not be taken lightly and needs to be well thought out. A major change in strategy may be required in three scenarios:

- *Customer needs change such that the core value proposition becomes obsolete*: Sometimes, as needs shift, companies can adapt. However, there are instances when the needs are no longer there. This can happen when structural changes in an industry shift and new needs emerge. For example, in the recorded music industry, cassettes replaced records, CDs replaced cassettes, and now streaming replaces all hard forms of recordings. Therefore, the need for music stores disappeared.

- *Innovation invalidates the essential activities of the value chain*: Dell's big advantage in selling PCs was its cost advantage of using a direct model. This strategy worked for two decades. Hewlett Packard, however, migrated to Taiwan outsourcing and eliminated Dell's cost advantage. Also, the rise in industry sales through the retail channel was a shift that also reduced Dell's advantages.

- *Technical breakthroughs can overwhelm the value proposition*: While truly disruptive technologies are rare, there are some striking examples. One example is digital photography. Kodak never made the investment in digital, and the one-hundred-year history of the most prominent photographic film manufacturer was reduced to bankruptcy.

When a strategy has worked well for an extended period, there is often tremendous resistance to making a change. Bias toward that strategy sets in, and leadership can become blind to the factors that make change so very necessary. This bias is a classic example of *escalation of commitment* (Vermeulen and Sivanathan, 2017). That is, leadership holds on too long to a once very successful strategy. Some not only hold on too long but also double down by ignoring or dismissing the concerns of those who see the tide changing and then continuing to invest heavily in the current strategy.

> When a strategy has worked well for an extended period, there is often tremendous resistance to making a change.

Nokia operated in the mobile communication business and became competitive in the early days. The situation changed when Apple introduced iOS (proprietary), and Google introduced Android OS (open source). These two smartphone introductions created a major impact to the competitive landscape. Nokia, however, was committed to its own proprietary operating system and doubled down on its investment. Subsequently, Samsung phones with Android OS and iPhones dominated the market in a relatively short time, while Nokia suffered and eventually sold its mobile phone unit. The Nokia story is a well-documented example of holding on to a good strategy too long (Potoroaca, 2022).

The aforementioned Kodak bankruptcy is another example of holding on to a strategy too long because of a need for more understanding of the change introduced into photography. The leadership did not believe that digital would advance in capability and in cost to be a serious competitor. They believed that films gave much higher-quality images, and that became their marketing theme. Also, they should have considered the convenience of digital for the amateur photographer. When smartphone cameras became a reality, the death knell for Kodak was clear.

HMV, the British music company, had an excellent strategy that worked amazingly well until the beginning of the new millennium. Their model was to operate music stores where customers could browse a large selection and listen to various artists before purchasing the compact disc (CD). Top management was warned that the industry was changing in various ways and that they should consider modifying their approach. The most serious change was the downloading and streaming of music. Their managing director, however, was even more committed to the existing strategy and was reported as saying, "Downloadable music is just a fad." HMV doubled down by continuing to invest in stores and kiosks. It was too late when they realized they needed to get into digital music. They subsequently went into receivership.

The studios thought they were in the movie business rather than the entertainment business and did not initially invest in television. In the movie studio case, they recovered in time to get a portion of the television industry.

What causes this escalation of commitment to a once successful strategy? There are various reasons (Vermeulen and Sivanathan, 2017):

- *Sunk costs*: When you have invested significant resources in a business venture that is not going well, there is a strong reluctance to stop and regroup. The loss that would occur causes a bias to believe that the situation will improve, even though objectively, it would be better to stop pouring more assets into a losing situation.

- *Loss aversion*: When there is a strong personal commitment and a loss that must be faced to change the strategic direction, be it a credibility loss or financial loss, many will resist changing direction. Research shows this bias is very strong.

- *Illusion of control*: Based on prior success with the strategy, many believe they will also be able to control the outcome in the future. That is, they believe the problem is not with the current strategy but with the implementation of the strategy that needs improvement.

- *Preference for completion*: Psychologically, many people want to stay the course and complete the project or continue on a given path, especially when it was successful in the past.

- *Pluralistic ignorance*: A situation where a decision is made for a group. All (or most) of the members of the group do not agree with the decision, but no one speaks up in dissent because each person believes they are the only dissenter. A classic example is the Abilene Paradox (Harvey, 1974), where a family drives from Coleman, Texas, to Abilene, Texas, on a hot (104°F) afternoon in a non-air-conditioned 1958 Buick.

All had gone along with the trip, but none of them truly wanted to take it. However, no one dissented at the outset.

- *Personal identification*: People identify with the decisions they make. There is a natural bias to promote those decisions and to avoid indications that the decision was wrong. So, decision-makers often ignore signs that the strategy is failing. This often leads them to double down on the strategic decision.

In 1985, Intel's core business was memory chips. It was their identity. Intel and memories were synonymous. After quite a successful run, Intel started losing money on memory chips because of the entry of high-quality, low-priced Japanese chips. Andy Grove and Gordon Moore, Intel's cofounders, were together discussing the memory chip issue (Grove, 1996), and Grove said, "Our mood was downbeat. I looked out the window and I asked, 'If we got kicked out and the board brought in a new CEO, what do you think he would do?' Gordon answered without hesitation, 'He would get us out of memories.' I stared at him, numb, and then said, 'Why shouldn't you and I walk out the door, come back, and do it ourselves?'" So, Intel overcame the resistance to change and boldly decided to concentrate on microprocessors. The rest is now history.

Takeaways: Stop Doubling Down on Your Losing Strategy

- The strategy should change if the customer needs change, the core value proposition becomes obsolete, innovation invalidates the essential activities, or a technological breakthrough overwhelms the value proposition.
- Recognize "escalation of commitment."
- Don't hold on too long to a strategy that was once successful.
- We need to recognize the changes in the industry and marketplace.
- Avoid escalation of commitment by addressing the following:
    - sunk cost fallacy
    - loss aversion
    - the illusion of control
    - pluralistic ignorance
    - personal identification
    - preference for completion
- Trust is so important to avoid this type of outcome.
- People need to be confident dissenters.

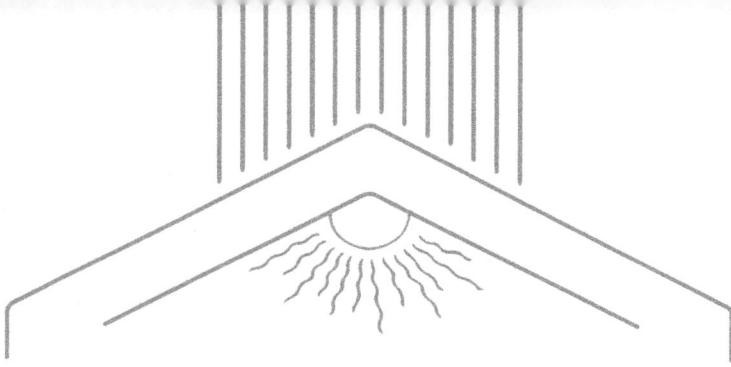

TOUCHSTONE # 42

A Business Either Grows or Declines; It Never Remains Constant

Most businesses don't remain stagnant for long. They either grow or shrink. There are several factors that contribute to this, such as the macroeconomic situation, trends in your business niche, and fluctuating demand for your products. You may also downsize your business by selling off underperforming divisions or discontinuing low-margin products. In any case, there are many variables that can impact your business, and it's important to recognize this and manage the changes effectively to ensure long-term success.

To establish a sustainable company, it is crucial to have a growth strategy with ambitious objectives. However, more important than that is cultivating a culture of growth with a competent leadership team (Schellinger, 2018). A company that does not grow fails to attract the most skilled individuals. To maintain a growth-oriented environment, it is essential to invest in people. A team of exceptional individuals will attract other talented people, creating opportunities for development and growth. Such a team will also provide the momentum to establish a growth-oriented value chain that aligns with the company's overarching strategy.

To keep this high-performing team challenged and engaged requires a strategy with bold strategic objectives. The team should be a significant part of developing these objectives. This is essential to retain such high-quality personnel. Of course, the incentives must be significant and match the challenges.

While you can do a lot of detailed analysis, developing high-growth plans requires some art. Having a deep understanding of your business and how it fits into the industry provides a feel for what is possible. This is key to sustaining growth. It is important to define the appropriate growth rate and how much you can stretch the growth objectives for your business. These stretch goals must be consistent with the industry and the market conditions you envision for the future. Setting unachievable goals will demoralize even the best people.

> To establish a sustainable company, it is crucial to have a growth strategy with ambitious objectives.

Trying to grow too fast will result in a lack of the necessary capital to maintain the growth. The business will become operationally stressed. Deadlines will be missed. Customers will be extremely disappointed and go elsewhere. The business will go into decline. On the contrary, if growth objectives are set too low, the company will be unable to support the customer base. The competitors will penetrate the company's business base, and the company will decline through loss of business. Therefore, the proper growth objectives must be put in place, with the appropriate amount of investment capital and the qualified team to execute the strategy.

Analysis in this area is difficult because there is such an interdependence among the specific company, the industry, the business cycle of the company's products or services, macroeconomic conditions, the competition, and customer needs. Analysis can help set a baseline, however. Financial analysts and investors use a metric to examine a company's basic growth capability at their current performance level. The sustainable growth rate (SGR) is the maximum company growth rate without borrowing additional capital or presenting operational hurdles. The SGR can theoretically be achieved by the business with the company's current margins, assets, debt ratios, and any dividend payments (Carlson, 2022). Calculating the SGR can help determine when you may need an infusion of cash and reduce the tendency to become overleveraged. The formula for sustainable growth rate is:

SGR = Retention Ratio x Return on Equity

where:

Retention Ratio = 1 – dividend payout ratio

Return on Equity = Net Income/Total Shareholder's Equity

SGR is an interesting guideline for mature companies and can help with capital structure and capital planning. The actual growth of the company is driven by culture, strategy, and capability. Of course, market conditions and competition also play a large part.

Takeaways: A Business Either Grows or Declines; It Never Remains Constant

- Observation: Businesses are rarely static for multiyear periods.
- Growing companies attract the best talent.
- The true growth capability is somewhat of an art form.
- It is important to define the appropriate growth rate for your company within the industry and its base of products.
- Trying to grow too fast results in a lack of capital, and the business will most likely become stressed and, therefore, decline.
- If growth objectives are too low, the competition will overtake you, and the business will decline through loss of business.
- SGR is the maximum company growth rate without borrowing additional capital, that is, without increasing leverage or debt. SGR is a guideline to help decide when a cash infusion is necessary. Actual growth is driven by:
    - growth strategy,
    - growth capability.
- The formula for sustainable growth rate is:
    - SGR = Retention Ratio x Return on Equity where:
    Retention ratio = 1 - (dividend payout ratio) and
    Return on Equity = Net Income/Total Shareholder's Equity.
    The retention ratio is the flip side of the dividend payout ratio.

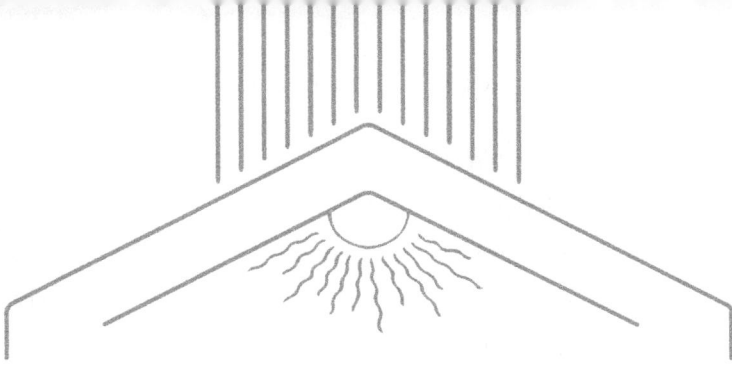

TOUCHSTONE #43

Assuming Your Competition Will Fail Is a Losing Strategy

You cannot build strength on the weaknesses of others.

You must focus on winning the business opportunity by providing greater value than the competition. As you compete for business with various companies, it is difficult to objectively assess how your company compares with the competition. As opposed to sports competitions, in business competitions, the rules of the game are not fixed. In sports, the criterion for winning is fixed. The football game winner is the team that scores the most points before the prescribed time runs out. There is some subjectivity in certain sports, such as gymnastics or figure skating, but the rules are clear. In contrast, competing for business can involve many factors and even the ability to change the rules during the competition. Therefore, your view of the competition may not be the customer's view.

Don't underestimate what your competitor might be able to do. *Can they bring on a teammate to shore up their weaknesses? Are they looking at a new technology to "leapfrog" your offering? Will they offer a unique business arrangement, such as bundling with other businesses to provide greater value?* There are several ways that the competitor may become more competitive or even try to unlevel the playing field without your knowledge.

An example of changing the playing field involved a customer that decided to put four products out to bid simultaneously; the winner takes all. This was envisioned as a five-year contract to manufacture all the requirements for these four products. These were highly technical, very difficult products to manufacture. There were four companies that could make the products, but none of the companies had yet to make all four products. Let's call them Companies A, B, C, and D.

> You cannot build strength on the weaknesses of others.

It was clear that Companies C and D were the weakest for this particular project and could not win the contract for several reasons. The industry experts predicted that the winner would be either Company A or B and permanently eliminate Companies C and D from this line of products.

Seeing this situation, Company C approached Company D with an interesting strategy. Company C manufactured two of the products, and Company D manufactured the other two. So, if they teamed, there would be no requalification necessary and no risk that there would be issues in producing all four of the products. The team could offer the customer a much lower-risk approach at a competitive price.

Companies C and D formed a joint venture company to submit a proposal, where they shared the potential profits fifty-fifty. Companies A and B had never built one of the products, which presented more risk for the customer. The customer awarded the contract to the joint venture company formed by Companies C and D. This shocked the industry experts (and Companies A and B), who had counted these companies out of the competition. So, you can never assume that your competitor will fail.

In 1999, two companies owned by Peter Thiel and Elon Musk were in intense competition (Thiel, 2014). They both had emerging products to facilitate rapid electronic payments for goods and services. Their products were very similar with little or no differentiation. By February 2000, both companies predicted that the dot-com bubble was likely to burst and ruin them. In March 2000, both leaders decided to merge their companies with a fifty-fifty deal that allowed them to survive the dot-com crash. The merged company, PayPal, became a major success story.

This discussion reinforces the concept that business strategy should not focus on the competition but on the customer. When you treat competition as a war, it is a destructive force. Typically, many stakeholders on both sides suffer. Creating superior customer value is the strongest competitive advantage you can have. This is the underpinning of a good business strategy. Furthermore, it can lead to the growth of an entire industry.

Business is not a zero-sum game. Companies that can create true value, especially with innovative products, can often open new growth for an entire industry. For example, look at what Amazon did. They took the Sears catalog model, modernized it with computer technology and rapid, reliable delivery, and expanded access to many consumers.

Finally, when looking at the competition, our natural bias and loyalty to our own company cause us to underestimate the competition's ability to perform. The competition will likely perform better than we expect.

Takeaways: Assuming Your Competition Will Fail Is a Losing Strategy

- One cannot build strength on the weaknesses of others.
- You must focus on winning the opportunity by providing greater value than the competition.
    - Remember to consider what your competitor might be able to do.
    - Ask yourself if the competitor is looking at a new technology to "leapfrog" your offering.
- Strategy should not be about the weaknesses of the competition.
- Strategy is about creating superior value for customers.
- Good business strategy is not a zero-sum game.
- Companies that create true value often open growth for an entire industry, not just their products. They expand the size of the pie.
- The competition will likely perform better than you expect.

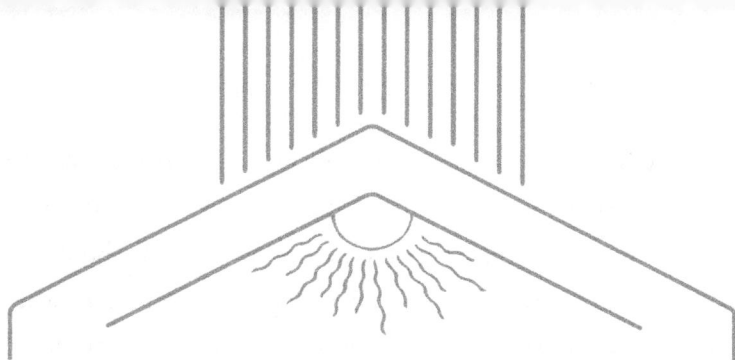

TOUCHSTONE #44

There Is No Upside without a Downside

Every opportunity to create an upside for your business, such as developing a new customer, launching a new product, implementing new technology, expanding your facilities, adding new talent, or acquiring a competitor, requires change.

With change come unknowns, and with unknowns comes risk. It often feels safer to go slow, to stay in your comfort zone. Without taking risks, however, the business will not perform to its potential. So, to be a successful business leader, it is essential to be able to move outside your safe zone and take calculated risks (Carosa, 2020). Now, the prudent leader will have evaluated what could go wrong and will have a risk mitigation plan and a backup action plan if the initial change plan starts to go awry. This backup plan is usually designed to avoid any potential significant downside.

When making a decision to take a calculated risk, it is often useful to ask, "What is the worst that can happen?" And then ask, "How likely is it to happen?" The answers to these questions will inevitably supply the basis for a risk mitigation plan but also trigger a risk-reward evaluation.

Faced with a proposition that will give the business an upside, such as implementing new technology, it is necessary to assess the value of the upside against the likelihood and cost of the downside risk. Let's suppose that the new technology will reduce production time and hence increase profits. The risk is that the technology will not work as well as you expect, or perhaps not at all. Therefore, the reward may be much less than expected, but you will still incur the full cost of implementing the new technology.

> If you assess the probability that the technology will fail to be very low and the reward very high, then you should probably take the risk since the odds are on your side that the upside will occur.

If you assess the probability that the technology will fail to be very low and the reward very high, then you should probably take the risk since the odds are on your side that the upside will occur. Of course, if the increased profits are small and the cost of the technology implementation is high, then the choice should be not to take the implementation risk. A risk mitigation approach may be to make a smaller investment and run a pilot program to check out the technology. If that works, then you can assess that the probability of the technology working at full scale will be much higher. This will bring the risk-reward equation back into balance, and you can implement the technology with higher confidence.

When formulating the business plan for the upcoming fiscal year, there will always be upside and downside potential. This is because there are inherent unknowns in the assumptions used to formulate the plan. The potential upsides and downsides can be evaluated in terms of risks and opportunities that can affect the plan. When creating the plan, it is helpful to list the major risks, the estimated probability of each occurring, and the financial impact should they occur. Likewise, list the opportunities, their probabilities, and their financial impact should they occur. These two tables set side by side will be extremely helpful in determining the overall confidence in the business plan. These will also help to generate a risk mitigation plan and reduce uncertainty for the upcoming year.

Finally, it is worthwhile to understand the systematic risks, those that affect the entire economy, and the unsystematic risks, those that affect your industry or your company.

Takeaways: There Is No Upside without A Downside

- Risk is inherent in business. We must accept that.
- Exploiting opportunities requires change; change involves unknowns; unknowns imply risk.
- No risk means no reward.
- The key to good planning is to balance the risk-reward equation.
- We must understand the risks and opportunities.
- When planning, assess the impact if the risk does not go in your favor.
- Likewise, assess the impact if the opportunity goes in your favor.
- Ask yourself if the probabilities of the downsides happening are similar to the probabilities of the upsides happening.
- Develop a risk mitigation plan.
- Reduce uncertainty as much as possible.
- Understand systematic versus unsystematic risk.

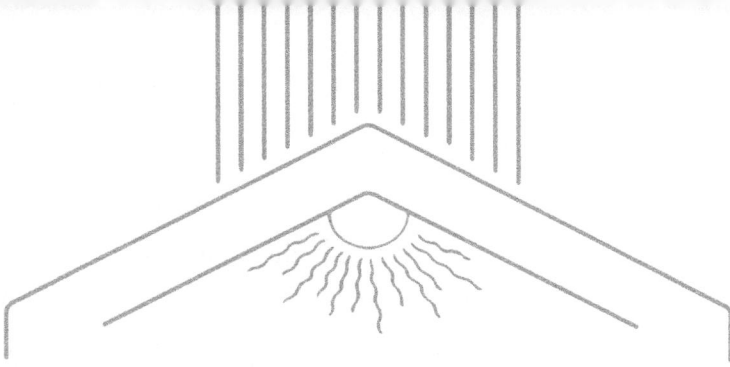

TOUCHSTONE #45

Simplicity Is the Crown of Genius; Complexity Is the Cloak of Mediocrity

Einstein has been quoted as saying, "The definition of genius is taking the complex and making it simple," while da Vinci wrote, "Simplicity is the ultimate sophistication."

Throughout history, great scholars have noted the power of simplicity. Today, we are constantly inundated with information, instant communication, and messages with inherent complexity. No one seems to take the time to communicate in clear, crisp, and simple ways. This tendency carries through to all aspects of life, especially in the business world, including products, processes, and presentations. The need for simplicity is strongly felt in all aspects of the business world and can be a source of competitive advantage (Lange, 2023).

Leaders who put forth simple, clear messages can move their organizations much more effectively toward a successful future. It is important to develop a culture of simplicity in the organization. Striving for simplicity is extremely important in the strategic planning process and in developing all aspects of business planning. People are intensely involved in their day-to-day work. The strategy needs to be simple for people to internalize it. Simplicity will also lead to improved decision-making with clear action plans. It will also breed efficiency, as there will be little need to correct errors caused by complex communications that are difficult to understand.

Business development activities will also benefit greatly from a focus on simplicity. Customer relationships can become stronger when the communications are direct with little or no ambiguity. Simplicity adds to credibility and trust when forging relationships. Complexity causes customers to pause and think, "What is this guy trying to hide?"

> Leaders who put forth simple, clear messages can move their organizations much more effectively toward a successful future.

Simple, straightforward proposals are usually more successful than those that are overly complex. The idea is to make it easier for the customer to understand the value you are creating and why your proposal is the lowest risk and most viable to meet the customer's need or solve the customer's problem. The simplest solutions are typically the most attractive.

Simplicity in product and process design has always been a fundamental principle of world-class design-for-manufacturability philosophy. A simpler design with fewer parts or process steps will always result in higher reliability and lower costs. It also involves having a straightforward supply chain that supports the company's manufacturing processes. When the supply chain for materials and related services becomes too complex, there is an increased risk of disruptions that may lead to quality or delivery problems.

A review of back-office processes can also benefit from a simplicity mindset. Payroll, personnel records, insurance, and many other business processes are prone to becoming complex over time. It is helpful to review them to see if they can be simplified.

It is useful to think of simplicity itself as a process. Whenever you address an issue related to your business, realize that you are only done once you find the simplest way to explain it, develop it, produce it, or use it. Of course, you must ensure that it is not simplified to an extent where it no longer meets its requirements. To quote Albert Einstein, "Everything should be made as simple as possible, but not simpler."

Takeaways: Simplicity Is the Crown of Genius; Complexity Is the Cloak of Mediocrity

- The power of simplicity applies to all aspects of the value chain.
- Great leaders strive to develop a culture of simplicity.
- Think of simplicity as a process. When you address an issue, you are only done once you find the simplest way to explain it, develop it, produce it, or use it.
- When something appears too complex, you will find mediocrity behind its development.
- Flow charts are excellent tools to identify unnecessary complexities.
- In presenting your ideas, sometimes it is necessary to reduce precision to accurately depict the situation.
- Simplicity wins in the long run. It survives, whereas complexity wanes.
- Einstein: "Everything should be made as simple as possible, but no simpler."

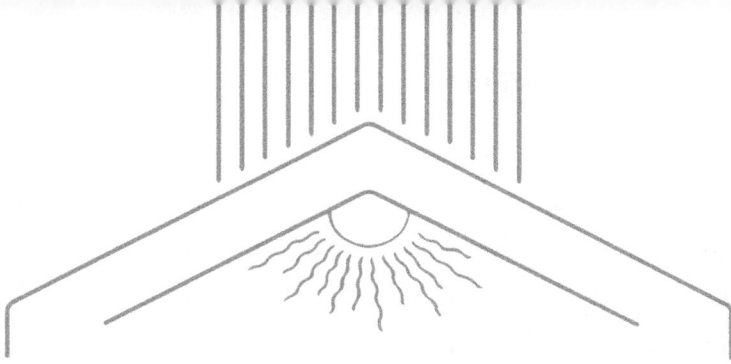

EPILOGUE

These Touchstones reveal a common theme or message: *great leadership is built upon trust and mutual respect.*

For a business to succeed in the long term, it must prioritize establishing trust and respect as integral parts of its fabric. To foster a unified culture within an organization, it is crucial to select individuals based on their strengths and talents and to build upon those strengths. The company must remain focused to align itself with its business strategy. Finally, perseverance is essential for achieving success.

Great business leaders are guided by a sense of realism. Being a *responsible realist* is crucial for business success. Being responsible entails adhering to ethical and legal standards, treating every individual fairly and respectfully, respecting the environment, maintaining honesty and openness in sales and marketing, ensuring safety in products, and providing safe working conditions. Being a realist acknowledges that the world is imperfect and accepts things outside their control as they are, using these realities to develop a business strategy that benefits all stakeholders in the business.

While each Touchstone has its individual or stand-alone value, organizing and connecting them through a logical leadership model demonstrate their collective value. Also, it exemplifies the power of the leadership model presented here to guide emerging leaders on their journey through the business world. Such a leadership model provides a road map for finding the right internal and external candidates to lead and manage the organization as it continues its journey toward becoming an outstanding player in its business area.

This model emphasizes that the foundation of good leadership is the ability to manage oneself. This is often lost on many leaders. There is a tendency for leaders to focus on training their staff on interpersonal skills and provide them with the modern aspects of developing relationships within the organization and concepts of emotional intelligence.

> Great leadership is built upon trust and mutual respect.

These aspects are very important and necessary for good leadership. However, if they are not supported by a solid foundation, that is, the ability to manage oneself, we will see those interpersonal skills wane and eventually become ineffective. This is because people will lose trust and respect in leaders without a strong foundation.

It is only possible to build a sound leader with a strong foundation.

There is a lot of literature on leadership and management. Recent literature has given more importance to the softer skills, which were not always emphasized by business leaders. The significance of these softer skills has been recognized more and more as a major factor in becoming a successful leader. The work on emotional intelligence by Goleman and the concept of Level 5 leadership brought forward by Collins, both based on significant research, opened the eyes of many business leaders. These leadership models have helped leaders to become more effective.

Finally, notwithstanding nor undermining their power, these Touchstones are not absolute in any way and are not rigid requirements. In a leadership role, nothing will replace good judgment

(Likierman, 2020). Good judgment must override all other guidance when making difficult decisions.

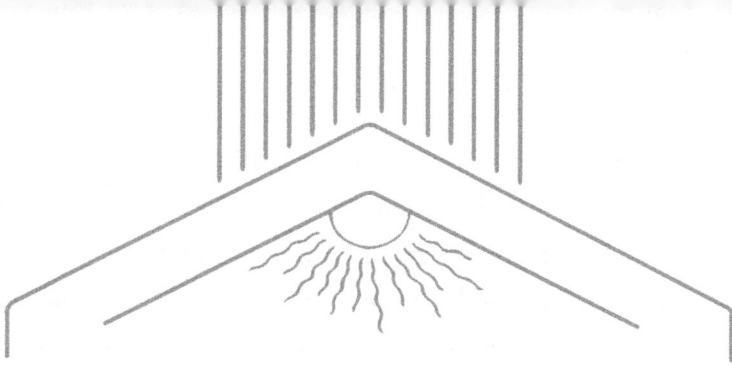

ABOUT THE AUTHOR

Joseph "Joe" Carleone was born in Philadelphia, PA where he attended Father Judge High School. After receiving his PhD from Drexel University, Joe helped start a company in the Aerospace and Defense industry, conducting R&D for the Department of Defense. He managed this business for nine years before being recruited to the West Coast by Aerojet.

For nearly twenty-five years, Joe held various leadership positions at Aerojet, including vice president of Tactical and Defense Rocket Motor Programs. He and his team developed military products that are still being produced today. Joe subsequently served as the vice president for Operations and also led the Remote Sensing Systems product sector, which marketed and delivered satellite sensors for surveillance, meteorological, and earth-sensing systems.

In 2000, Joe was appointed president of Aerojet Fine Chemicals which developed, scaled, and produced Active Pharmaceutical Ingredients (APIs) for the pharmaceutical industry. Joe led the sale of Aerojet Fine Chemicals to American Pacific Corporation (AMPAC), thereafter serving as Chairman and CEO. He subsequently led the take-private of AMPAC with H.I.G. Capital and remained on as CEO.

Over the course of his career, Joe has served as a Member of the International Ballistics Committee and the National Defense Industrial Association, Chairman of the Ballistics Division of the National

Defense Industrial Association, and an Executive Board Member of the Insensitive Munitions & Energetic Materials Division. He has been a member of the American Society of Mechanical Engineers, American Institute of Aeronautics and Astronautics, American Chemical Society, and the Board of Governors of the Aerospace Industries Association. He was also a board member of the Arthritis Foundation.

At Drexel University, the Joseph and Shirley Carleone Endowed Fellowship Fund was established to provide assistance to PhD students. Joe was inducted into the Drexel 100 and named to Drexel's College of Engineering Alumni Circle of Distinction. He currently serves on the Dean of Engineering's Advisory Council.

Joe has also been named to the World Association Co-op Hall of Fame and the Father Judge High School Hall of Fame. He received the Firepower Award from the Picatinny Chapter of the NDIA. Joe has published over forty-five articles and a book entitled *Tactical Missile Warheads*. Joe also developed a course on business leadership, presented to senior executives, which led to *The Touchstones of Leadership*.

He is currently Chairman of Avid Bioservices and Lead Director of Sensient Technologies, and further serves as a senior advisor to OES Europe, specializing in trans-Atlantic M&A.

Joe and his wife Shirley have two daughters and four grandchildren, and call southern Nevada home.

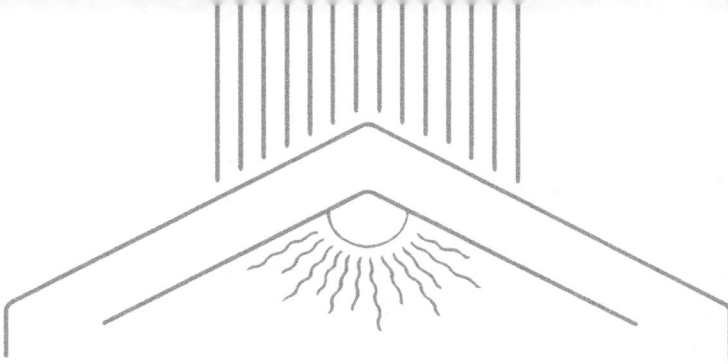

BIBLIOGRAPHY

Amabile, Teresa, and Steve Kramer. "Valuing your most valuable assets." Harvard Business Review. October 2011. https://hbr.org/2011/10/valuing-your-most-valuable

Atiyeh, Clifford. "Everything you need to know about the VW diesel-emissions scandal." Car and Driver. November 13, 2015. https://www.caranddriver.com/news/a15339250/everything-you-need-to-know-about-the-vw-diesel-emissions-scandal/

Atkinson, John W. *An Introduction to Motivation*, D. Van Nostrand Company, Inc, 1965, Oxford: Van Nostrand, 1964. ISBN 0-442-20367-5

Bacon, Brian. "Intuitive intelligence in leadership." Oxford Leadership. 2015. https://www.oxfordleadership.com/intuitive-intelligence-in-leadership/

Bailey, James R. "The best managers are leaders—and vice versa." September 22, 2022. Harvard Business Review. https://hbr.org/2022/09/the-best-managers-are-leaders-and-vice-versa

Bamforth, Mark. Pharma's Almanac, Q1 2020, Volume 6, Number 1, page 5.

Beaty, Roger E. and Yoed N. Kenett. "Mapping the Creative Mind." *American Scientist* 168, no. 4 (2020): 219–224.

Brafman, Ori, and Rom Brafman. *Sway: The Irresistible Pull of Irrational Behavior*. New York: Doubleday, 2008. ISBN: 978-0-385-52438-4

Buckingham, Marcus, and Curt Coffman. *First, Break All the Rules: What the World's Greatest Managers Do Differently*. Simon & Schuster, 1999. ISBN: 0-684-85286-1

Bunker, Kerry A., Kathy E. Kram, and Sharon Ting. "The young and the clueless." Harvard Business Review. December 2002. Reprint R0212F.

Calzon, Bernardita. "A complete guide on how to set smart KPI targets and goals." The datapine Blog. June 22, 2022. www.datapine.com/blog/kpi-targets-goals-examples/

Carlson, Rosemary. "Sustainable growth for a business." The Balance. September 13, 2022. https://www.thebalancemoney.com/what-is-the-sustainable-growth-for-a-business-393231

Carosa, Chris. "Why successful entrepreneurs need to be calculated risk takers." Forbes. August 7, 2020. https://www.forbes.com/sites/chriscarosa/2020/08/07/why-successful-entrepreneurs-need-to-be-calculated-risk-takers/

Catlette, Bill, and Richard Hadden. "Feed the opportunities, starve the problems." Contented Cow Partners. December 11, 2013. https://contentedcows.com/blog-item-48-feed-the-opportunities-starve-the-problems/

Catmull, Ed. "How Pixar fosters collective creativity." Harvard Business Review. September 2008. https://hbr.org/2008/09/how-pixar-fosters-collective-creativity

Cholle, Francis P. *The Intuitive Compass*. San Francisco: Jossey Bass, 2012.

Chu, Angela Hsin Chun, and Jin Nam Choi. "Rethinking Procrastination: Positive Effects of 'Active' Procrastination Behavior on Attitudes and Performance." *Journal of Social Psychology* 14 (2005): 245–264.

Collins, Jim. *Good to Great*. New York: Harper Business (HarperCollins), 2001. ISBN: 0-06-662099-6

Collins, Jim. *Turning the Flywheel*. London: Random House Business Books, 2019.

Covey, Stephen M. R. *The Speed of Trust*. New York: Free Press (Simon & Schuster), 2006. ISBN-13: 978-0-7432-9730-1

Covey, Stephen R. *Principle-Centered Leadership*. New York: Fireside (Simon & Schuster), 1992. ISBN: 0-671-74910-2

Covey, Stephen R. *The Seven Habits of Highly Effective People*. New York: Free Press, 1989. ISBN: 0-7432-6951-9

Creelman, James. "Forecasting and target-setting: they are NOT the same thing." 2017. https://www.linkedin.com/pulse/ forecasting-target-setting-same-thing-james-creelman

Day, Sherri. "Coke makes up with Burger King over rigged test of frozen drink." New York Times. August 2, 2003. https://www.nytimes. com/2003/08/02/business/coke-makes-up-with-burger-king-over-rigged-test-of-frozen-drink.html

Demers, Jayson. "How to change your mindset to see problems as opportunities." July 1, 2015. https://www.inc.com/jayson-demers/how-to-change-your-mindset-to-see-problems-as-opportunities.html

Dhingra, Naina, Andrew Samo, Bill Schaninger, and Matt Schrimper. "Help your employees find purpose—or watch them leave." https://www. mckinsey.com/capabilities/people-and-organizational-performance/ our-insights/help-your-employees-find-purpose-or-watch-them-leave, April 5, 2021.

Drucker, Peter F. *The Effective Executive*. New York: HarperCollins Publishers, 2006.

Drucker, Peter F. "Managing oneself." Harvard Business Review. January 1999. https://hbr.org/2005/01/managing-oneself

Drucker, Peter F. "The five deadly business sins." Wall Street Journal. October 21, 1993. https://www.wsj.com/articles/SB10001424052748704204304574544283192325934

Eisenstein, Paul A. "Takata pleads guilty for cover-up related to airbag deaths." February 27, 2017. https://www.nbcnews.com/business/autos/takata-plead-guilty-cover-related-airbag-deaths-n726196

Eksteen, Danie. "Intuition as a leadership tool—it's like having the world wide web in your head." University of Stellenbosch Business School. June 19, 2019. https://usb-ed.com/blog/

Engelberg, Moshe. "Marketing 101: if you can't fix it, feature it." San Diego Physician, August 2005.

Ferrante, Steve. "Why champions don't have time to procrastinate," web, October 2018.

Fisher, Roger, William Ury, and Bruce Patton. *Getting to Yes*. New York: Penguin Books, 3rd Edition, 2011.

Fox, Erica A. *Winning from Within*. New York: HarperCollins, 2013.

Gesmer, Lee. "Trial practice: if you can't fix it, feature it (or at least mention it before the other side does)." May 14, 2011. https://www.masslaw-blog.com/trials-2/trial

Goleman, Daniel. "What makes a leader?" Harvard Business Review. June 1996. https://hbr.org/2004/01/what-makes-a-leader

Gordon, Barry and Lisa Berger. *Intelligent Memory*. New York: Viking, Penguin Group, 2003.

Green, Melanie. "Why is it so stressful to talk politics with the other side?" The Conversation. April 6, 2018. https://theconversation.com/why-is-it-so-stressful-to-talk-politics-with-the-other-side-92391

Greer, Michael. "Why it's pointless to argue about politics or religion." Worth Sharing. 2015. https://worthsharingessays1.pressbooks.com/chapter/

Grove, Andrew S. *Only the Paranoid Survive.* New York: Currency (Bantam Doubleday Dell), 1996.

Harvey, Jerry B. "The Abilene Paradox: The Management of Agreement." *Organizational Dynamics* 3, (1974): 63–80. doi: 10.1016/0090-2616974090005-9

Janis, Irving Lester. *Groupthink: Psychological Studies of Policy Decisions and Fiascoes.* New York: Houghton Mifflin Company, 1982.

Jennings, Marianne M. *The Seven Signs of Ethical Collapse: How to Spot Moral Meltdowns in Companies … Before It's Too Late.* New York: St. Martin's Press (Macmillan), 2006.

Kahneman, Daniel, Dan Lovallo, and Olivier Sibony. "Before you make that big decision." Harvard Business Review. June 2011a. https://hbr.org/2013/06/before-you-make-that-big-decision

Kahneman, Daniel. *Thinking, Fast and Slow.* New York: Farrar, Straus, and Giroux, 2011b.

Kraaijenbrink, Jeroen. "The ten myths of strategy." March 15, 2019. https://www.forbes.com/sites/jeroenkraaijenbrink/2019/03/15/the-ten-myths-of-strategy/

Kraaijenbrink, Jeroen. *The Strategy Handbook.* New York: Simon & Schuster, 2022.

Kraus, Elizabeth. "Do you really treat employees like you treat your best customers?" March 2017. https://marketingdesks.com/treat-employees-like-your-best-customers

Lange, Charles. "The power of simplicity: how embracing simplicity at every level of business and marketing can drive success." Medium. March 29, 2023. https://medium.com/@charleslangeconsultant/the-power-of-simplicity-how-embracing-simplicity-at-every-level-of-business-and-marketing-can-ae52c312a80d

Levitin, Daniel. *The Organized Mind.* New York: Penguin Random House, 2014.

Lieberman, Matthew D. "Should leaders focus on results, or on people?" Harvard Business Review. December 27, 2013a. https://hbr.org/2013/12/should-leaders-focus-on-results-or-on-people

Lieberman, Matthew D. *Social: Why Our Brains Are Wired to Connect.* New York: Crown Publishers, 2013b. ISBN 978-0-307-88909-6

Likierman, Sir Andrew. "The elements of good judgement." Harvard Business Review. January-February 2020. https://hbr.org/2020/01/the-elements-of-good-judgment

Livingston, J. Sterling. "Pygmalion in management." Harvard Business Review. January 2003. https://hbr.org/2003/01/pygmalion-in-management

Luntz, Frank I. *Win: The Key Principles to Take Your Business from Ordinary to Extraordinary.* New York: Hyperion, 2011. ISBN: 978-1-4013-2399-8

Magretta, Joan. *Understanding Michael Porter.* Boston: Harvard Business Review Press, 2012.

Martin, Roger L. "How successful leaders think." Harvard Business Review. June 2007. https://hbr.org/2007/06/how-successful-leaders-think

Oncken, William, Jr., and Donald L. Wass. "Management time: who's got the monkey?" Harvard Business Review. November 1999. https://hbr.org/1999/11/management-time-whos-got-the-monkey

Plungis, Jeff. "Volkswagen used special software to exaggerate fuel-economy claims, EPA says." Consumer Reports. August 30, 2019. https://www.consumerreports.org/fuel-economy-efficiency/volkswagen-used-special-software-to-exaggerate-fuel-economy/

Porath, Christine, and Christine Pearson. "The price of incivility." Harvard Business Review. January-February 2013. https://hbr.org/2013/01/the-price-of-incivility

Porter, Michael E. "From competitive advantage to corporate strategy." Harvard Business Review. May-June 1987. https://hbr.org/1987/05/from-competitive-advantage-to-corporate-strategy

Porter, Michael E. "What is strategy?" Harvard Business Review. November-December 1996. https://hbr.org/1996/11/what-is-strategy

Porter, Michael E. *On Competition, Updated and Expanded Edition*. Harvard Business Review Book Series, 2009.

Potoroaca, Adrian. "Nokia: the story of the once-legendary phone maker." November 24, 2022. www.techspot.com/article/2236-nokia/

Riazi, Atefeh. "Keeping those who hate you away from those who are undecided." June 2022. https://medium.com/@atti-riaz/keeping-those-who-hate-you-away-from-those-who-are-undecide-1119746ff8da

Richards, Bill. "New data on asbestos indicate cover-up effects on workers." The Washington Post. November 12, 1978. https://www.washingtonpost.com/archive/politics/1978/11/12/new-data-on-asbestos-indicate-cover-up-of-effects-on-workers/028209a4-fac9-4e8b-a24c-50a93985a35d/

Robinson, Jack K. "Do not be afraid of hard work." January 8, 2013. https://jackrobinson.com/do-not-be-afraid-of-hard-work/

Roosevelt, Theodore. "The man in the arena," excerpt from "Citizen in a Republic," speech April 23, 1910, delivered at the Sorbonne, Paris, France.

Rosenthal, Robert, and Lenore Jacobson. *Pygmalion in the Classroom.* New York: Holt, Rinehart, and Winston, 1968, p. 11.

Rumsfeld, Donald. *Rumsfeld's Rules.* New York: HarperCollins, 2013.

Schellinger, Mark. "In business, you're either growing or you're dying." March 23, 2018. https://www.forbes.com/sites/forbeslacouncil/2018/03/23/in-business-youre-either-growing-or-youre-dying/

Schwartz, Tony, and Catherine McCarthy. "Manage your energy, not your time." Harvard Business Review. October 2007. https://hbr.org/2007/10/manage-your-energy-not-your-time

Simmons Hanly Conroy Team. "Asbestos litigation history: the cover-up." May 21, 2013. https://www.simmonsfirm.com/blog/asbestos-litigation-history-the-cover-up/

Skitka, Linda J. "The Psychology of Moral Conviction." *Social and Personality Compass* 4, no. 4 (2010): 267–281.

Skitka, Linda J., Brittany E. Hanson, G. Scott Morgan, and Daniel C. Wisneski. "The Psychology of Moral Conviction." *Annual Review of Psychology* 72, (2021): 347–366.

Smith, Ned. "Who says creativity can't be learned?" Business News Daily. May 7, 2012. https://www.businessnewsdaily.com/2471-creativity-innovation-learned.html

Solow, Daniel. "In Models We Trust—But First, Validate." *American Scientist* III, January-February 2023.

Thiel, Peter. *Zero to One*. New York: Currency, an imprint of Crown Publishing, 2014.

Thorndike, William N., Jr. *The Outsiders*. Boston: Harvard Business Review Press, 2012.

Vermeulen, Freek, and Niro Sivanathan. "Stop doubling down on your failing strategy." Harvard Business Review. November-December 2017. https://hbr.org/2017/11/stop-doubling-down-on-your-failing-strategy

Voss, Chris. *Never Split the Difference: Negotiating as If Your Life Depended on It*. New York: HarperCollins, 2016.

Zenger, John H., and Joseph Folkman. *The Extraordinary Leader: Turning Goal Managers into Great Leaders*. New York: McGraw-Hill, 2009.

Zidarić, Željko. "Being respected or being liked—which do you strive for as a leader?" December 9, 2015. https://www.linkedin.com/pulse/being-respected-liked-which-do-you-strive-leader-zeljko-zed-zidaric/

Zitelmann, Rainer. "What focus really means: learning from Bill Gates, Warren Buffett and Steve Jobs." Forbes, October 28, 2019. https://www.forbes.com/sites/rainerzitelmann/2019/10/28/what-focus-really-means-learning-from-bill-gates-warren-buffett-and-steve-jobs/

www.ingramcontent.com/pod-product-compliance
Lightning Source LLC
Chambersburg PA
CBHW031502180326
41458CB00044B/6670/J